W9-CQS-008

BIG
Book of
$5.00
Crafts™

Edited by Laura Scott

HOUSE of
WHITE
BIRCHES
PUBLISHERS
SINCE 1947

Big Book of $5.00 Crafts

Copyright © 2001 House of White Birches, Berne, Indiana 46711

All rights reserved. No part of this publication may be reproduced or transmitted in any form or by any means, electronic or mechanical, including photocopying, recording, or any other information storage and retrieval system, without the written permission of the publisher.

Editor: Laura Scott
Technical Editor: Lâna Schurb
Associate Editor: Cathy Reef
Copy Editor: Mary Nowak
Publications Coordinators: June Sprunger, Tanya Turner

Photography: Tammy Christian, Jeff Chilcote, Justin P. Wiard
Photography Stylist: Arlou Wittwer
Photography Assistant: Linda Quinlan

Production Coordinator: Brenda Gallmeyer
Graphic Arts Supervisor: Ronda Bechinski
Book/Cover Design: Jessi Butler
Graphic Artist: Amy S. Lin
Production Assistants: Janet Bowers, Marj Morgan
Traffic Coordinator: Sandra Beres
Technical Artists: Leslie Brandt, Julie Catey, Chad Summers

Publishers: Carl H. Muselman, Arthur K. Muselman
Chief Executive Officer: John Robinson
Marketing Director: Scott Moss
Book Marketing Manager: Craig Scott
Product Development Director: Vivian Rothe
Publishing Services Manager: Brenda R. Wendling

Printed in the United States of America
First Printing: 2001
Library of Congress Number: 00-109645
ISBN: 1-882138-69-4

Every effort has been made to ensure the accuracy and completeness of the instructions in this book. However, we cannot be responsible for human error or for the results when using materials other than those specified in the instructions, or for variations in individual work.

Ready, Set, Craft!

Dear Crafters,

Have you ever heard of someone who can go to a large craft store and spend only a few dollars? Neither have I! Anytime I visit our local craft stores, I bring home enough supplies to stock a smaller store in my basement! (One of these days my husband will catch on! Until then …)

In this jam-packed idea book, we bring you a creative collection of craft-it-yourself projects, each of which you can make for under $5.

"How can that be?" you ask.

Well, much of the secret to keeping crafting affordable lies in making sure you make the most of each supply you purchase. For this book, though we may show only one sample of an item, with the materials you purchase, you should be able to make several of that item—perfect for craft fairs and gift-giving! This will bring your cost per item, in some cases, well below $5!

We've also included many projects that use recycled items. It is truly amazing how you can turn a simple glass bottle into a sensational decoration or gift!

All of these projects are terrific for selling at bazaars, decorating your home, and giving as gifts for special friends and family.

Warm regards,

Laura Scott

We know you'll enjoy crafting and sharing each of these delightful yet inexpensive-to-make projects with family and friends!

Sunshine Gifts

Craft It, Wear It!

Bazaar Fun

Holiday Accents

Sunshine Gifts

Spread a little sunshine by crafting delightful and sure-to-be-appreciated gifts for celebrations all year-round! From birthdays to baby showers to holidays and get-well wishes, you're sure to find just the right "special something" for family and friends at an affordable cost to you!

"Get Well" Birdies

Send a cheerful bluebird with your good wishes to brighten the day of an ailing friend with a cute gift tote, bag tag and very special get-well card.

Designs by Annie Lang

Let's Begin!

Materials
Each Project
- PeelnStick double-sided adhesive sheets from Therm O Web
- Black fine-tip permanent marking pen
- Tracing paper
- Americana acrylic paints from DecoArt: titanium white #DA1, pineapple #DA6, antique gold #DA9, true blue #DA36, lamp black #DA67, Indian turquoise #DA87, ultra blue deep #DA100 and petal pink #DA214
- Paintbrushes: ¼" and ½" angle shaders , #2 and #5 pointed rounds, size 4 and 10 flat shaders and size 0 liner (optional)
- Matte-finish spray sealer
- Round paper punch
- Decorative paper edgers

Gift Tote & Tag
- Brown (10½" x 8") corrugated cubby handle bag
- 9" x 12" sheet 140-lb. watercolor paper
- 1 sheet Cheerful & Charming decorative paper from Hot Off the Press or other decorative paper
- 30" (¼"-wide) pink satin ribbon

Greeting Card
- 1 sheet white card stock
- 9" x 12" sheet 140-lb. watercolor paper
- Heavy brown paper bag
- Silver fine-tip marking pen

Project Notes

Refer to photo and patterns (page 10 and 11) throughout.

Use tracing paper to transfer design by using technique described in "Using Transfer Paper" in General Instructions on page 191.

This project is "coloring book" painted: Simply fill in areas with paint as directed, as if you were coloring the pages of a coloring book. Areas will then be "floated" with shading and outlined with pen.

See instructions for floating under "Painting Techniques" in General Instructions on page 191.

Use the brushes to fit the areas you are painting. Angular shading brushes are used to float shading colors. Flat shaders are used to block in areas of color. Round brushes are used to paint dot patterns on clothing. Liner is for fine details.

Gift Bag

1. Transfer patterns for gift bag birdie and gift bag heart onto watercolor paper.

2. *Bird body:* Paint with Indian turquoise. When dry, float with thinned true blue. Use #5 round brush to tap thinned petal pink onto cheek areas. Paint beak and feet pineapple; float edges with antique gold. Add tiny white highlight dots to cheeks; add white highlight strokes to beak and feet.

3. *Gown:* Leave unpainted, but float edges with thinned true blue shading. Paint undiluted true blue collar, cuffs and hemlines. When dry, shade sleeve cuffs and area under hemline near feet (underside of gown) with ultra blue deep. Add polka dots of undiluted true blue to gown.

4. *Heart:* Leave unpainted, but float edges with petal pink.

5. When paints have dried, add lettering and border and detail lines with black marking pen; let dry thoroughly.

6. Lightly mist painted surfaces with two or three coats of sealer, allowing sealer to dry between coats.

7. Apply a sheet of adhesive to wrong side of decorative paper; using decorative paper edgers, cut a 6 ¼" square. Remove paper backing to expose adhesive and press square firmly onto center of bag's front side, using your fingernail to press the paper into the bag's corrugated grooves.

8. Press a sheet of adhesive onto wrong side of heart and bird. Without removing paper backing, cut out bird; set aside. Remove paper backing from adhesive on heart and affix a piece of decorative paper to back of heart; cut out heart shape and punch two holes where indicated.

9. Remove paper backing from bird; press onto front of bag over decorative paper; he should tilt slightly upward as if hovering.

10. *Attach hanging heart:* Using craft knife, poke two tiny holes through front of bag, one just above where finger and thumb meet on extended arm and the other just under small finger. Cut a 12" piece of ribbon and thread through holes so ends dangle outside front of bag. Tie ends through holes in heart, making sure

Continued on page 10

"Get Well" Birdies continued from page 8

that right side of heart faces you. Cut a 6" piece of ribbon; tie in a bow around ribbon hanger just below bird's hand.

Bag Tag

1. Transfer pattern for bag tag birdie onto watercolor paper.

2. Paint bird and heart shape as directed in steps 2–5 for gift bag. Float edges of background rectangle with petal pink. When dry, load round brush with petal pink and tap brush up and down on palette to work paint into bristles. Gently tap color here and there throughout background, using an up-and-down pouncing motion.

3. Detail tag and apply sealer as directed in steps 5 and 6 for gift bag.

4. Apply a piece of decorative paper to back of bag tag with piece of adhesive sheet. Cut out bag tag and punch corner in upper left corner.

5. Tie tag to bag handle or other gift with a 12" piece of pink ribbon tied in a bow through hole in tag.

Greeting Card

1. Transfer patterns for card cover and card interior onto watercolor paper.

2. Paint birds' bodies, gowns and heart as directed in steps 2–4 for gift bag.

3. *Background:* Float edges of background rectangles with petal pink. When dry, load round brush with petal pink and tap brush up and down on palette to work paint into bristles. Gently tap color here and there throughout background, using a pouncing motion.

4. *Thermometer and frame on cover:* Using silver pen throughout, add border to greeting card cover. Fill in bulb of thermometer and add a few marking lines.

5. When paints have dried, add lettering and border and detail lines with black marking pen; let dry thoroughly.

6. Lightly mist painted surfaces with two or three coats of sealer, allowing sealer to dry between coats.

7. Apply adhesive to back of painted card cover and interior; cut out rectangles.

8. Fold card stock in half and trim with scissors to make a 5" x 7" greeting card.

9. From heavy brown paper, cut a 5" x 7" rectangle (cover) and a 4½" x 6" rectangle (interior); back each with adhesive sheet. Trim ¼" from all edges of rectangles with paper edgers. Remove backing and apply smaller rectangle so it is centered on card interior (not over fold) and larger one centered on cover.

10. Peel backing from adhesive and affix painted cover design to center of brown paper on cover; repeat with painted design for card interior on inside of card. ❀

Card Interior

Card Cover

Gift Bag Birdie

Something to Cheer You!

Bag Tag Birdie

Get Well!

Gift Bag Heart

Something to Cheer You!

Get Well!

Teddy Bear Switch Plate

Teddy bear fans of all ages will adore this creative and simple decorative accent. For a child's room, consider a complementary pastel for the main color of the switch plate.

Design by Mary Ayres

Let's Begin!

Materials

- 5¼" x 6¼" single wooden switch plate
- Wooden products from Forster Inc.: 2½"-diameter disk, 1¾"-diameter disk, 4 craft stick minis, 3 Woodsies (¾"-diameter) circles, Woodsie (1¼"-diameter) circle, Woodsie (⅜"-diameter) circle, and 2 Woodsies (1½") ovals
- ½" x 1" wooden primitive heart from Lara's Crafts
- Americana acrylic paints from DecoArt: country red #DA18, antique white #DA58, sable brown #DA61, lamp black #DA67, light cinnamon #DA114, light buttermilk #DA164, and golden straw #DA168
- Glorious gold #DA71 Dazzling Metallics acrylic paint from DecoArt
- #6 and #8 round bristle paintbrushes
- ZIG twin-tip black permanent marker from EK Success Ltd.
- ⅜ yard (⅞"-wide) plaid ribbon
- Tacky craft glue
- Plastic wrap
- Seam sealant (optional)
- Hair dryer (optional)

Project Notes

Refer to photo and pattern throughout.

Refer to directions for dry-brushing and rouging under "Painting Techniques" in General Instructions on page 191. Let all paints and ink dry between applications.

Instructions

1. Paint switch plate antique white.

2. In a small container mix half-capful light buttermilk with half-capful water; paint front and sides of switch plate with mixture. While still wet, dab surface with a wad of scrunched-up plastic wrap until desired texture is achieved. Air dry or blow dry with hair dryer.

3. Dry-brush edges of switch plate with glorious gold.

4. Draw words on right side of switch plate with fine tip of marker.

5. Paint primitive heart country red; dry-brush edges with glorious gold. Add highlight dot in upper right with paintbrush handle dipped in light buttermilk. Glue heart to switch plate between L and V.

6. Using sable brown, paint all surfaces of both wooden disks, two ¾" circles, all craft stick minis and ovals; paint ¾" circle and 1¼" circle with golden straw; paint ⅜" circle lamp black. Dry-brush edges of all painted bear pieces with light cinnamon.

7. *Head (1¾" disk):* Rouge cheeks with country red. Glue on muzzle (golden straw ¾" disk); glue nose (black ⅜" disk) to upper center of muzzle. Add highlight dot to center of each cheek and nose with paintbrush handle dipped in light buttermilk. Draw eyes with side of marker's bullet tip.

8. Using fine tip of marker, draw blanket stitch stitches around edges of all painted bear pieces except nose.

9. Glue ovals (feet) to ends of two craft stick minis (legs); glue legs and remaining craft stick minis (arms) to front of switch plate. Glue body (2½" disk) on top of arms and legs. Glue ears (sable brown ¾" circles) to back of head; glue head to switch plate above body.

10. Tie ribbon in a bow and trim ends even; notch ends and treat with seam sealant if desired. Glue bow to bear's neck. ✤

Teddy Bear Switch Plate

Bear Country Boxes

"Cabin-style" decor is hot, hot, hot, and this duet fits the look perfectly! Paint, wooden cutouts and ribbon trim transform miniature papier-mâché boxes into a black bear and his brown cousin.

Designs by Mary Ayres

Let's Begin!

Materials
Both Bears

- ☐ 2 (2½" x 3½") oval papier-mâché boxes with lids from D&CC
- ☐ ⅞"-wide ribbon: ⅜ yard blue-and-green plaid and ⅜ yard blue with white polka dots
- ☐ Wooden products from Forster Inc.: 2 (1¾"-diameter) disks; 4 Woodsies (¾"-diameter) circles; 4 Woodsies (⅜"-diameter) circles
- ☐ Round wooden furniture plugs: ¾" and ½"
- ☐ Americana acrylic paints from DecoArt: white wash #DA2, country red #DA18, antique white #DA58, sable brown #DA61, lamp black #DA67, light cinnamon #DA114 and camel #DA191
- ☐ #6 and #8 round bristle paintbrushes
- ☐ ZIG markers from EK Success Ltd.: black fine-tip permanent marker and mocha 0.5mm extra-fine-tip opaque writer
- ☐ Tacky craft glue
- ☐ Seam sealant (optional)

Project Notes

Refer to photo and patterns (page 16) throughout.

Refer to directions for dry-brushing and rouging under "Painting Techniques" in General Instructions on page 191.

Let all paints and ink dry between applications.

Black Bear

1. Using lamp black, paint exterior surfaces of one box and lid, as well as ¾" furniture plug (nose) and two ¾" circles (ears). Using camel, paint two ⅜" circles (inner ears) and one 1¾" disk (muzzle).

2. Using light cinnamon, dry-brush edges of all pieces painted in step 1.

3. Rouge cheeks on box lid with country red. Using tip of paintbrush handle dipped in white wash, dot on eyes, cheek dots and highlight on nose.

4. Using black marker, dot pupils onto white eyes; add dashed line around edge of muzzle, and straight mouth line up center of muzzle; add dashed lines around edges of inner ears.

5. Glue muzzle and ears to box lid. Glue nose to muzzle and inner ears to ears. Let dry.

6. Using mocha writer, add dots randomly over all black surfaces on lid and sides of box to indicate fur.

7. Tie polka-dot ribbon in a bow; trim ends and treat with seam sealant if desired. Glue bow to top of box lid, centering bow under muzzle.

Brown Bear

1. Using sable brown, paint exterior surfaces of

Continued on page 16

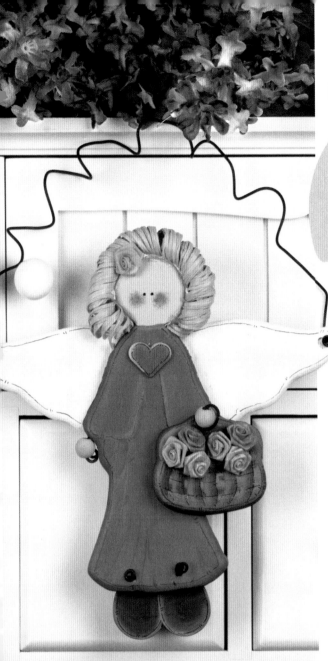

Garden Angel

An inexpensive ready-made angel is easy to dress up with paints and other materials.

Design by June Fiechter

Let's Begin!

Materials

- ☐ 7" wooden angel #9133-26 from Provo Craft
- ☐ Woodsies ⅞" wooden heart from Forster Inc.
- ☐ 2" x 2" wooden heart cutout
- ☐ 2⅜" x 2" wooden basket cutout
- ☐ 2 (⅜"-diameter) wooden beads
- ☐ 6" strand coiled natural raffia hair
- ☐ Ceramcoat acrylic paints from Delta: flesh-tone #2019, lavender #2047, berry red #2056, GP purple #2091, dark flesh #2127, cinnamon #2495, and white #2505
- ☐ Fine-point black permanent marking pen
- ☐ Raf-a-doodles 100 percent Natural Curled Raffia from One & Only Creations
- ☐ 7 (½") ribbon rosettes in a combination of three complementary pastels
- ☐ 16-gauge craft wire
- ☐ Small paintbrush
- ☐ Small stencil brush
- ☐ Hot-glue gun
- ☐ Wood glue
- ☐ Craft drill with small bit
- ☐ Scrap wood
- ☐ Screwdriver
- ☐ Wire cutters
- ☐ Needle-nose pliers

Project Notes

Refer to photo throughout.

Let all paints and ink dry between applications.

Refer to directions for rouging and highlighting under "Painting Techniques" in General Instructions on page 191.

Instructions

1. Pry halo off angel using screwdriver.

2. Lay pieces atop a piece of scrap wood and drill holes: Drill a hole through tip of each wing for adding hanger. Drill a hole through top center of basket and another from front to back of angel near bottom of right sleeve where basket will be attached later (drill through both layers of angel—body and wings). Drill two holes at bottom of angel for attaching feet and two corresponding holes through larger wooden heart cutout. Drill a hole about ½" into edge of angel at

bottom of left sleeve where left hand will be attached.

3. Paint all surfaces of basket and larger wooden heart (feet) with cinnamon; highlight edges of feet, edges of basket and basket weave pattern with dark flesh. Paint beads and angel's head with flesh-tone; paint all surfaces of wings white. Paint all surfaces of gown lavender; highlight with purple along edges and to define sleeves. Paint smaller heart cutout berry red; highlight edges with fleshtone.

4. Rouge cheeks lightly with berry red using small stencil brush. Using black marking pen, dot on eyes and add an outline of lines and hash marks around wings, basket, robe and feet; add final definition to pattern of basket weave.

5. Coiling and kinking wire with needle-nose pliers, attach wire hanger, feeding ends through holes in wings from back to front and coiling ends tightly on front to hold hanger in place. Attach feet at bottom of angel with two small pieces of wire, coiling ends tightly on front and back to hold feet in

place. Kink one end of a short piece of wire; thread on bead and test fit in hole for left arm; trim wire as needed and hot-glue straight end in hole. Thread wooden basket, then remaining bead on another piece of wire; attach to right arm, coiling wire tightly on front and back to hold pieces in place.

6. Glue coil of curled raffia over top of angel's head, trimming as necessary. Glue one silk rosette to hair and head at top left.

Glue remaining rosettes to top of basket. Glue berry red heart to center front of angel's gown. ❀

Bear Country Boxes *continued from page 14*

one box and lid, as well as ½" furniture plug (nose) and two ¾" circles (ears). Using antique white, paint two ⅜" circles (inner ears) and one 1¼" disk (muzzle).

2. Using light cinnamon,

dry-brush edges of all pieces painted in step 1.

3. Repeat steps 3–7 as for black bear, substituting plaid ribbon for polka-dot ribbon. ❀

Black Bear

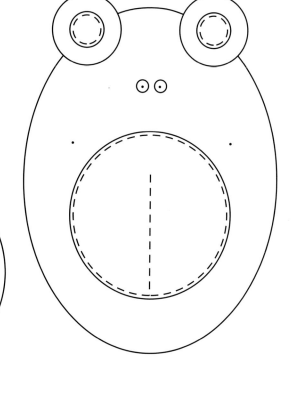

Brown Bear

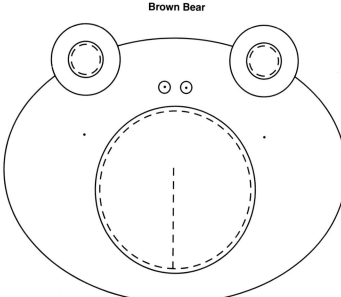

Monogrammed Note Cards

Choose colors and patterns of decorative paper to create anything from formal stationery to whimsical personalized notes.

Designs by Mary Ayres

Let's Begin!

Materials
Each Note Card

- 5¾" x 4⅜" parchment card with matching envelope from Rubber Stampede
- Yasutomo decorative papers: Fold'ems Metallic Origami Paper, Folk Art Patterns patterned paper, and specialty paper
- Black card stock
- 8½" x 11" sheet computer paper
- ZIG Memory System black fine-tip permanent marker from EK Success Ltd.
- 48-point (½") commercial script press-on lettering
- Pinking shears
- Glue stick

Project Notes

Refer to photo throughout. The 48-point press-on lettering is the largest size available. Unfortunately, it is not large enough for the card monogram, which is why it is necessary to scan it into the computer and enlarge it. Enlarging a type font already in the computer will not work; the edges of the enlarged type have a squared look.

Instructions

1. Decide on a pleasing combination of parchment card, black card stock, and patterned and metallic papers.

2. Cut 4" x 5¼" rectangle from black card stock; glue to center front of card.

3. Cut a 3½" x 4½" rectangle from patterned paper; glue to center of black rectangle.

4. Cut a 2½" x 3¼" rectangle from metallic paper; glue to center of patterned rectangle.

5. *Monogram:* Press desired press-on letter onto center of computer paper. Scan into computer. Enlarge it to 200 percent and print on specialty paper.

6. Using a pencil, draw 1¼" x 1¾" rectangle on specialty paper with enlarged letter in center of rectangle. Go over pencil outline with fine-tip black marker.

7. Lightly pencil another rectangle around the first, ¼" larger on all sides. Cut around outside edge of this larger rectangle with pinking shears. Erase all pencil lines and glue pinked monogram rectangle in center of metallic rectangle. ❧

"Bee Happy!" Gift Bag

Perfect for nearly all gift-giving occasions, this paper tote is a snap to make with the help of a ready-made transfer and a few other simple materials you probably have on hand right now.

Design by June Fiechter

Let's Begin!

Materials

- ☐ 8" x 10" brown paper gift bag with handles
- ☐ 5½" x 7½" corrugated kraft paper or cardboard
- ☐ White card stock: 4½" x 5¼" rectangle and 6¾" x 2½" strip
- ☐ Heavy brown paper: 2⅞" x 2⅜" and 1⅜" x 2¼" rectangles
- ☐ Decorative paper edgers
- ☐ Home Accents Busy as a Bee transfer #41-8482 from Provo Craft
- ☐ Ceramcoat Sparkle Glaze from Delta
- ☐ Black medium-point permanent marking pen
- ☐ Craft glue
- ☐ Small paintbrush
- ☐ Several strands of fine natural raffia
- ☐ Round paper punch

Project Notes

Refer to photo throughout.

Refer to manufacturer's instructions for applying transfers.

Instructions

1. Trim edges of card-stock pieces with paper edgers.

2. Transfer beehive with two bees to center of larger brown paper rectangle. Glue to bottom portion of larger piece of white card stock. Using black marking pen, write "Bee Happy!" on top area of card stock.

3. Glue corrugated paper rectangle to center of one side of gift bag. Center decorated card stock atop corrugated paper and glue in place.

4. Paint a light coat of sparkle glaze over transfer and onto card stock.

5. *Gift tag:* Transfer single bee to center of smaller piece of brown paper. Fold card stock strip in half; glue decorated brown paper to center of one side. Paint front of gift card with sparkle glaze.

6. Write message inside gift tag. Punch hole in upper left corner and tie to handle of gift bag with a bow of several fine strands of natural raffia. ✿

Mini Gift Box Duo

Add extra punch to a tiny gift when you enclose it in a one-of-a-kind keepsake box. Ready-made papier-mâché boxes are inexpensive and fun to paint!

Designs by Laura Scott

Let's Begin!

Materials

Round Box

- [ ] 4" round papier-mâché box with lid
- [ ] FolkArt acrylic paints from Plaid Enterprises: bright baby pink #223, yellow lemon #226, violet pansy #440, magenta #412 and titanium white #480
- [ ] Fun-to-Paint Dotters from Plaid Enterprises: daisy #50106 and single dot #50112

Heart Box

- [ ] 4" heart-shape papier-mâché box with lid
- [ ] FolkArt acrylic paints from Plaid Enterprises: violet pansy #440, magenta #412, school bus yellow #736 and fresh foliage #954
- [ ] Fun-to-Paint Dotters from Plaid Enterprises: tulip #50104 and triple dot #50111

Each Box

- [ ] Sandpaper
- [ ] Lint-free cloth
- [ ] #12 flat paintbrush
- [ ] Spray sealer

Project Notes

Refer to photo throughout.

Allow sealer and paints to dry thoroughly between coats.

General instructions follow; refer to individual instructions for detailed directions on painting designs.

Instructions

1. Lightly sand box and lid. Dampen cloth slightly and wipe off dust. Apply sealer to exterior surfaces of box and lid.

2. *Base coat:* Apply two or three coats of base color to box and lid as directed for individual designs below, using sufficient coats for complete coverage.

3. *Apply paint with dotter:* Squeeze small amount of specified color(s) onto paper plate or other palette. Apply paints as directed with dotters.

4. Spray box and lid, inside and out, with one or two coats of sealer.

Painting Round Box

1. *Base-coat exterior:* Apply magenta to sides and bottom of box and top of lid. Apply violet pansy to side of lid.

2. *Base-coat interior:* Paint inside of box and lid bright baby pink.

3. *Apply paints with dotters:* Using daisy dotter, paint titanium white daisies on lid top and box side, gently "rolling" dotter to paint petals evenly. Add yellow lemon center to each daisy with single dotter.

Painting Heart Box

1. *Base-coat exterior:* Apply school bus yellow to sides and bottom of box and top of lid. Apply violet pansy to side of lid.

2. *Base-coat interior:* Paint inside of box and lid fresh foliage.

3. *Apply paints with dotters:* Using tulip dotter, paint magenta tulips on lid top and box side, gently "rolling" dotter to paint tulips evenly. Using triple dotter, add clusters of three fresh foliage dots between tulips on lid top and box sides, and on violet pansy edge of lid. ✿

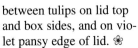

"Baby's Asleep" Door Hanger

Let everyone know that it's naptime by hanging this sweet and simple reminder made of craft foam from the nursery doorknob. And what a nice baby shower gift!

Design by Barbara Matthiessen

Let's Begin!

Materials

- ☐ Craft foam: 5" squares pink and light brown
- ☐ Fabri-Tac glue from Beacon Adhesives
- ☐ ZIG markers from EK Success Ltd.: 0.5mm black marker and red and brown pigment ink markers
- ☐ White acrylic craft paint
- ☐ 12" piece (8mm) white cord
- ☐ ½" pink ribbon rosette with green ribbon leaves
- ☐ 12" piece (¼"-wide) pink satin ribbon
- ☐ Tiny flat white button
- ☐ Small, stiff stencil brush or fabric-painting brush
- ☐ Round hole punch

Project Note

Refer to photo and patterns (page 22) throughout.

Instructions

1. Cut heart from pink foam. Cut one bear head, two ears and four paws from light brown foam.

2. Shade edges of heart by rubbing red marker along edge for a few inches, then using stiff bristle brush to spread ink toward center. In same manner, shade edges of light brown pieces with brown marker.

3. Blush cheeks, inner ears and paw pads by rubbing bristle end of brush across red marker, then rubbing in a circular motion onto foam to achieve lighter shading.

4. Using black marker, add outline around edge of heart and lettering.

Outline all bear pieces; add dot eyes, then triangular nose and vertical muzzle line. Add paw pad details to paws.

5. Add three highlight dots at top of each cheek using toothpick dipped in white paint.

6. Punch two holes for attaching hanger in top of heart ¼" from edge. Glue paws to front of heart; glue bottom edge of head to back of heart at center top; glue ears to back of head.

7. Glue ribbon rosette to top of head. Tie ribbon in a bow; glue at center top of heart. Glue white button over center of bow.

8. *Hanger:* Thread ends of cord through holes, leaving ends protruding from front; knot ends. ❀

Templates continued on page 22

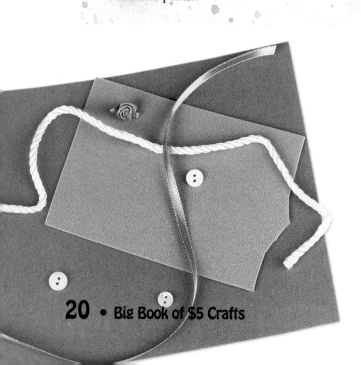

Cutie Pie Floor Cloth

This painted canvas floor cloth is a charming addition to a nursery or children's bath. Paint it up from start to finish in just a couple of hours!

Design by Paula Bales

Let's Begin!

Materials

- 21½" x 27" piece heavy canvas
- Americana acrylic paints from DecoArt: titanium white #DA1, pineapple #DA6, hi-lite flesh #DA24, baby pink #DA31, baby blue #DA42, mint julep green #DA45, and wisteria #DA211
- 1½" wave Fun to Paint Shape Tape from Plaid Enterprises
- Paintbrushes: wash, angular wash and spotter
- Fabric glue
- Exterior/interior varnish
- Household sponge
- Pencil with new eraser
- Straight pin

Project Notes

Refer to photo and patterns (page 22) throughout.

Follow manufacturer's instructions for using Fun to Paint Shape Tape.

When dotting on paint, use the end of a wooden paintbrush handle unless instructed otherwise.

Let all paints and varnish dry between applications.

Instructions

1. Fold under edges of canvas ½"; glue in place with fabric glue.

2. Position 1" wave tape 2" from short ends of floor cloth and ½" tape 4" from ends of floor cloth.

3. Paint ends of floor cloth pineapple; top with randomly placed single mint julep green dots and clusters of three wisteria dots.

4. Paint next sections wisteria; add random dots of titanium white.

5. Paint large center section mint julep green. Add single titanium white dots, slightly larger single baby pink dots, and clusters of three small pineapple dots. Center a smaller dot of lamp black in each baby pink dot.

6. Carefully remove wave tape. Paint 1" wave baby blue and ½" wave baby pink. Using the head of a straight pin, add a tiny lamp black dot in each curve of baby pink waves. Add narrow lamp black lines across curves of baby blue waves; add baby pink dots between black lines.

7. Cut shape of head from household sponge. Dampen sponge slightly, then dip into hi-lite flesh and press onto mint julep green section of floor cloth for each face, sponging a total of six faces.

8. *Paint three toothy grins and three big grins:* Paint cheeks baby pink. Dot on eyes with lamp black using the eraser end of pencil. Paint teeth titanium white. Paint eyebrows, lashes and mouths—and outline teeth—with lamp black. Add tiny white highlight dots to eyes with head of pin. Dot on baby pink noses.

9. Coat painted surface with varnish. ✿

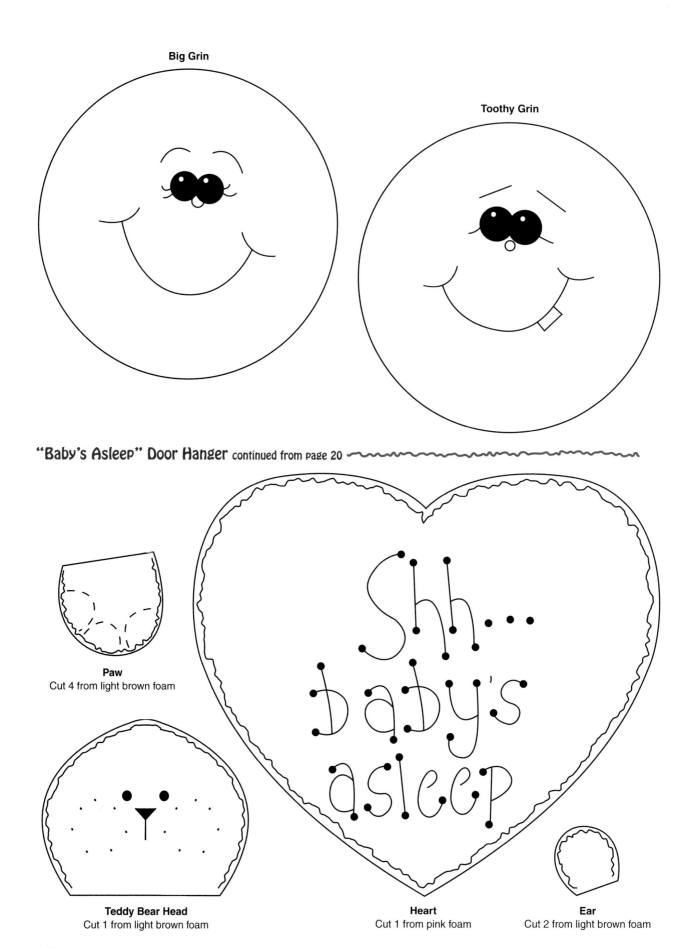

Big Grin

Toothy Grin

"Baby's Asleep" Door Hanger continued from page 20

Paw
Cut 4 from light brown foam

Shh...
baby's
asleep

Teddy Bear Head
Cut 1 from light brown foam

Heart
Cut 1 from pink foam

Ear
Cut 2 from light brown foam

Baby Bottle Bank

It's never too early to start saving for college, and this whimsical baby bottle will make it easy to start stashing that spare change.

Design by Annie Lang

Let's Begin!

Materials

- Glass or plastic baby bottle with nipple and cap
- Tracing paper
- Graphite paper
- Ultra Gloss air-cure paints from DecoArt: gloss white #DG1, gloss black #DG2, and royal fuchsia #DG55
- Paintbrushes: #8 pointed round and size 0 liner

Project Notes

Refer to photo and pattern throughout.

Let all paints dry between applications.

When completely cured, painted bottle will be dishwasher safe. Follow paint manufacturer's recommendations.

Instructions

1. Trace pattern onto tracing paper. Place graphite paper on work surface with dark graphite side up. Place traced design over graphite paper and retrace lines with pencil.

2. Choose flattest unprinted area of bottle. Tape pattern in place over this area on bottle. Retrace over pattern lines with pencil to transfer design to bottle.

3. Using #8 round brush through step 5, paint eyes gloss white. Apply a second coat for good coverage.

4. Paint heart-shaped cheeks, nose and tongue royal fuchsia.

5. Paint inner mouth and pupils gloss black.

6. Using liner brush through step 7, add tiny gloss white highlight dots to each cheek and to center of nose.

7. Outline and add details with gloss black.

8. Cut off top of rubber nipple. With nipple still attached to bottle, push remaining rubber part of nipple to inside of bottle to hide cut edges and create slot. ❧

Baby Bottle Bank

"It's a Girl!" Baby Announcement

Perched on a plant stake, this colorful design is a delightful addition to a gift basket, a warm welcome home for Mom and the newest little miss. Or, skip the plant stake and add a ribbon hanger to suspend from doorknob or door wreath.

Design by June Fiechter

Let's Begin!

Materials

- Precut wooden snowman shape from Provo Craft
- ¼"-diameter wooden dowel
- Ceramcoat acrylic paints from Delta: flesh-tone #2019, pretty pink #2088, Sonoma wine #2446, fuchsia #2481, white #2505, blue lagoon #2528 and Caribbean blue #2530
- ¼" paintbrush
- Hot-glue gun
- Medium-point black permanent marker
- ⅝"–¾" flat wooden button
- Satin exterior/interior varnish

Project Notes

Refer to photo throughout.

Refer to directions for base-coating and rouging under "Painting Techniques" in General Instructions on page 191.

Instructions

1. Base-coat one side of snowman shape with fleshtone. Add a second coat if necessary for complete, smooth coverage.

2. Paint cap blue lagoon; paint bows fuchsia; paint hair Sonoma wine. Use as many coats as necessary for even, complete coverage. Paint wooden button blue lagoon.

3. Rouge cheeks using pretty pink. Dot on eyes with paintbrush handle dipped in Caribbean blue.

4. Using medium-point marker, outline all sections

Continued on page 26

Keepsake Tooth Pocket

Save Baby's first tooth in this sweet keepsake pocket stitched in pink or blue. It's also a nice place to keep that lost tooth safe under the pillow until the tooth fairy can make a trade.

Design by Helen Rafson

Let's Begin!

Materials

- ☐ White felt from Kunin Mfg.
- ☐ Fusible interfacing
- ☐ Air-soluble marker
- ☐ 2 (½"-diameter) flat pink or blue buttons
- ☐ 12" piece (⅜"-wide) pink or blue satin ribbon
- ☐ 6½" piece (¼"-wide) pink satin ribbon (for girl's tooth pocket only)
- ☐ DMC 6-strand embroidery floss: pink #899 or blue #334
- ☐ Sewing thread: coordinating pink or blue
- ☐ Needle
- ☐ Seam sealant

Project Notes

Refer to photo and patterns (this page and page 26) throughout.

Follow manufacturer's instructions for using fusible interfacing.

Instructions

1. From white felt cut two teeth and one tooth pocket; cut one tooth pocket from fusible interfacing.

2. Using air-soluble marker, write child's name where indicated by line on tooth pocket pattern. Using 3 strands floss, backstitch name and, below it, the word "TOOTH."

3. Fuse interfacing to wrong side of stitched pocket.

4. Using 4 strands embroidery floss, blanket-stitch across top edge of fused tooth pocket. Lay two felt teeth together; lay pocket on top, matching edges. Pin layers together and blanket-stitch around edges through all layers with 4 strands embroidery floss.

5. Sew buttons to top of tooth using coordinating thread.

6. Treat ends of ⅜"-wide ribbon with seam sealant. When dry, sew ends to back of tooth with coordinating thread for hanging loop.

7. For girl's tooth pocket, tie ¼"-wide ribbon in a bow; cut ends at an angle and treat with seam sealant. When dry, sew bow to center top with coordinating pink thread. ❀

Stitch name along this line

TOOTH

Tooth Pocket
Cut 1 from white felt
and 1 from fusible interfacing

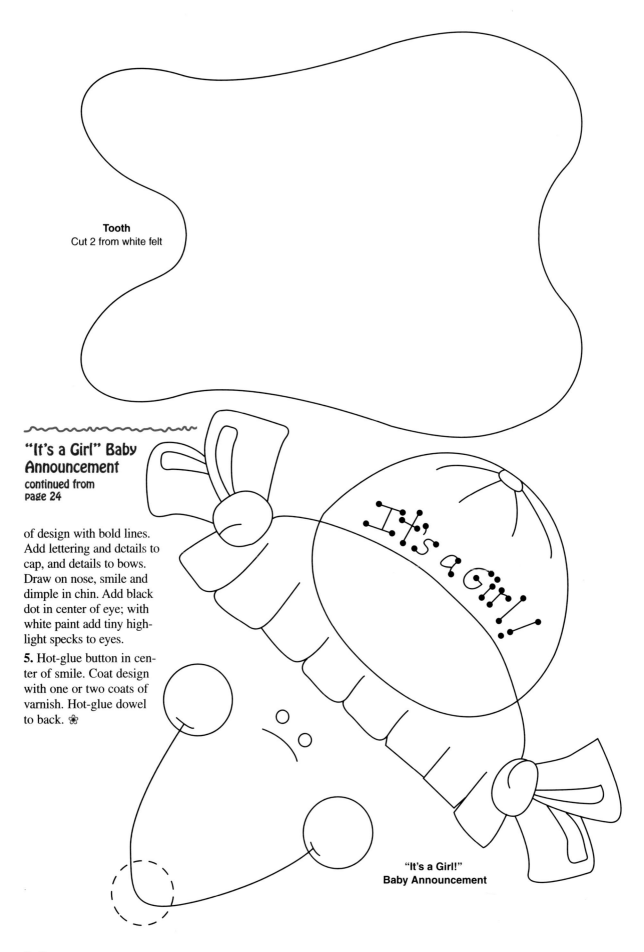

Tooth
Cut 2 from white felt

"It's a Girl" Baby Announcement
continued from page 24

of design with bold lines. Add lettering and details to cap, and details to bows. Draw on nose, smile and dimple in chin. Add black dot in center of eye; with white paint add tiny highlight specks to eyes.

5. Hot-glue button in center of smile. Coat design with one or two coats of varnish. Hot-glue dowel to back. ❧

"It's a Girl!"
Baby Announcement

Potpourri Teapot

Add a quaint Victorian touch to a guest bath or boudoir with this beribboned wicker "teapot" filled with an aromatic "brew" of your favorite dried potpourri!

Design by Bev Shenefield

Project Notes

Refer to photo throughout.

Let gesso and paints dry between applications.

Yardages and amounts may vary depending on the size of your wicker teapot or other wicker object.

Instructions

1. Using filbert brush through step 2, paint teapot and lid, inside and out, with gesso.

2. Mix equal amounts ivory and ultra white paints; paint pot and lid, inside and out, with mixture.

3. *Paint knob on teapot lid:* Mix three parts fuchsia with one part light burgundy; combine two parts of this mixture with one part ultra white and apply mixture with flat brush.

4. Place lid on pot; mark position of handle on lid. Beginning at this point, turn under end of lace and cement it around outer edge of lid. When you reach starting point, trim off excess, leaving enough to again turn under the end before cementing it in place.

5. Glue ¾" ribbon rosette to knob on lid. Space smaller ribbon rosettes evenly around top edge of lace on lid.

6. *Potpourri bag:* Place dry potpourri in center of tulle circle; gather tulle around potpourri and tie securely with ribbon. Insert potpourri bag in teapot. ❀

Let's Begin!

Materials

- ☐ Wicker teapot
- ☐ 14" piece beading lace strung with rose ribbon
- ☐ Rose ribbon rosettes with green ribbon leaves from Offray: 7 (½") and 1 (¾")
- ☐ 10½" circle ivory or white tulle
- ☐ 12" piece ivory or rose ribbon
- ☐ Dried rose potpourri
- ☐ Craft cement
- ☐ Gesso from Delta
- ☐ CeramDecor PermEnamel paints from Delta: light burgundy #45009, fuchsia #45013, ivory #45020 and ultra white #45029
- ☐ Paintbrushes: filbert size ¾ and flat size 8

Wedding Sachet Gift Bags

Fill these adorable bags with lavender or birdseed to shower on the guests—or fill with aromatic potpourri and present the sachets as gifts to the bridal party and others who help make the special day unforgettable.

Design by Phyllis Sandford

Let's Begin!

Materials

Set of Three Sachets

- 3 sachet bags from BagWorks
- Starlite Shimmering fabric paints from Delta: sachet pink #438 and leaf green #439
- Sparkling cranberry #512 Glitter fabric paint from Delta
- Stencil Buddy #508
- Cherished Memories Borders & More from Delta: romantic #614 and wedding #623
- Stencil adhesive spray from Delta
- 3 sprigs of dried stardust gyp
- Heavy cardboard
- 3 (7") strands white pearl beads-by-the-yard
- (12") strands ⅛" double-faced satin ribbon from Wright's: 3 wine and 3 light green
- Dried lavender, birdseed or other stuffing
- Monogram Magic Sentiments from Delta: Love #061

Project Notes

Refer to photo throughout.

Refer to manufacturer's instructions for using all stenciling products.

Apply all paints with small piece of foam and Stencil Buddy, and change foam for each color. Remember that a little paint goes a long way. Tap off extra paint onto a piece of paper toweling before applying paint to fabric.

Instructions

1. Spray backs of stencils with spray adhesives. (Do not spray back of Sentiments stencil; it already has a sticky back.)

2. Position one of the designs toward bottom of each stencil bag; press into place.

3. Cut a small piece of cardboard to fit inside each sachet bag to hold front of bag smooth and taut (this will keep paint from leaking through to other side).

4. *"Love" Sachet:* Using romantic border, stencil large word "Love" with sachet pink, hearts with sparkling cranberry and

Continued on page 30

Gilded Books Candle Holder

Everyone has a few unwanted books lying around. Transform them into a glittering decoration that will dress up a table delightfully for a graduation celebration —or a party congratulating a new author!

Design by June Fiechter

Let's Begin!

Materials

- ☐ 3 hardcover books
- ☐ Pale gold #DM01 Royal Metallics textured paint from DecoArt
- ☐ Foam paintbrush
- ☐ 2 (1⅝"-high, 1¼"-diameter) wooden candle cups
- ☐ 2 gold or white taper candles
- ☐ 2 (1") wood screws
- ☐ Craft drill with bit to fit screws
- ☐ 1 yard (2¼"-wide) white voile or tulle ribbon with metallic gold wired edges
- ☐ Dried baby's breath
- ☐ Tacky craft glue

Project Notes

Refer to photo throughout.

Take extreme care when burning candles; never leave burning candles unattended.

Instructions

1. Paint covers of books, including inner edges, and exterior surfaces of candle cups with textured gold paint. Glue books together in a stack.

2. Wrap ribbon around books widthwise, ribbon ends on top. Tie in a bow and/or arrange ribbon ends in a pleasing arrangement. Trim ribbon as desired.

3. Using craft drill and wood screws, attach painted candle cups to center top of books; add sprigs of baby's breath between and around candle cups and ribbon streamers.

4. Insert candles in candle cups. ✿

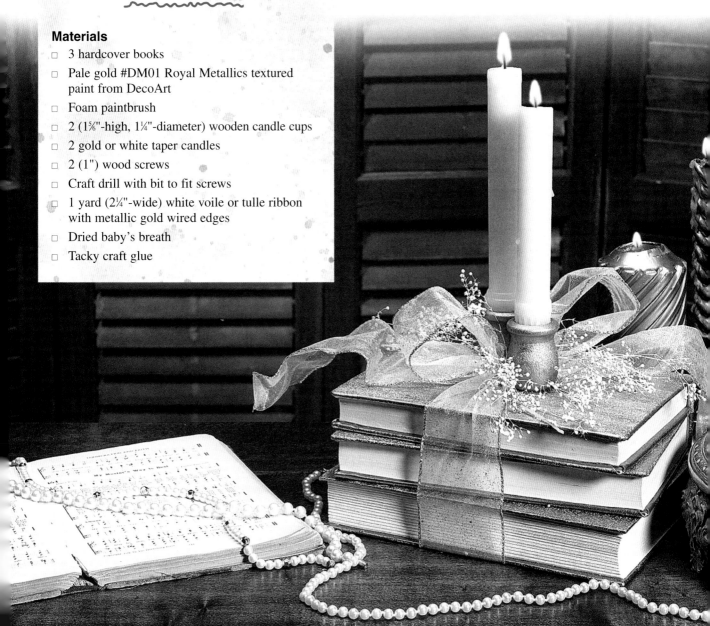

Vintage Buttons Pincushion

Look into your button jar for a few favorites to decorate this stylish bureau-top pin minder.

Design by Barbara Woolley

Let's Begin!

Materials

- 4½" heart-shaped papier-mâché picture-frame box from D&CC
- 3" x 14" piece PeelnStick double-sided adhesive from Therm O Web
- 2 coordinating fabrics: 3" x 14" strip of fabric A and 6" square of fabric B
- Coordinating acrylic paint
- Small paintbrush
- Clear matte or satin varnish
- Permanent adhesive
- Assorted buttons
- Polyester fiberfill

Project Notes

Refer to photo throughout.

Refer to manufacturer's instructions for using double-sided adhesive.

Instructions

1. Paint entire box with acrylic paint in selected color. When dry, coat with a thin, even coat of varnish.

2. Apply double-sided adhesive to wrong side of fabric strip. Peel off paper backing, then apply fabric to sides of box.

3. Glue a handful of fiberfill to center of flat, heart-shaped insert portion of frame lid. Lay 6" square of fabric over fiberfill; glue fabric to edges of insert. Trim excess fabric.

4. Glue insert into frame; fabric-covered fiberfill should puff up in frame.

5. Glue buttons onto frame with permanent adhesive. ❁

Wedding Sachet Gift Bags continued from page 28

flowers with leaf green. Using a toothpick, place a dot of sparkling cranberry in center of each flower.

5. *Hearts Sachet:* Using wedding border, stencil one heart with sachet pink and the other with sparkling cranberry. When dry, position Sentiments stencil below hearts and

stencil "Love" with sparkling cranberry.

6. *Bouquet Sachet:* Using wedding stencil, position flowers with bow on sachet. Stencil bow with sachet pink, flowers with sachet pink and sparkling cranberry, and stems and leaves with leaf green. Using a toothpick, place a

dot of sparkling cranberry or stencil pink in center of each flower. When dry, position Sentiments stencil below hearts and stencil "Love" with sachet pink.

7. Fill bags with desired stuffing.

8. Tie a piece of wine ribbon and light green ribbon

around top of each sachet; tie in a bow. Tie a strand of pearls around center of bow, positioning a sprig of dried gyp between ribbons. ❁

Happy Birthday Papaw!

Youngsters will enjoy helping with this special gift for a very special person! Have fun playing with the details to increase the resemblance to your "Papaw," then fill the can with some favorite treats, pens, pencils—or perhaps a fishing lure or two.

Design by Paula Bales

Let's Begin!

Materials

- ☐ Empty 4½"-tall tin can with one end removed, washed, dried, and any sharp edges filed smooth
- ☐ 1½" x 12" torn strip of coordinating fabric
- ☐ Off-white metal primer
- ☐ Americana acrylic paints from DecoArt: buttermilk #DA3, base flesh #DA136, and tomato red #DA169
- ☐ Tulip black slick paint
- ☐ Paintbrushes: wash and #4 bristle
- ☐ Black fine-point permanent marker
- ☐ 22-gauge wire
- ☐ Wire cutters
- ☐ Dried Spanish moss
- ☐ 4" piece cut from straight end of a wooden paint-stirring stick
- ☐ 9½" (³⁄₁₆"-diameter) wooden dowel
- ☐ ZIG .5mm bluebell Woodcraft Marker from EK Success Ltd.
- ☐ Craft cement
- ☐ Hot-glue gun
- ☐ Household sponge

Project Notes

Refer to photo throughout.

Let all paints and ink dry between applications.

Instructions

1. Spray inside and outside of can with two coats of metal primer.

2. Using sponge, dab base flesh over entire exterior surface of can.

3. Using tomato red and a pouncing motion, paint cheeks.

4. Paint eyes with black slick paint; add tiny highlight dot to each with buttermilk paint.

5. Using fine-point black marker, draw eyebrows and mouth.

6. Glue clumps of Spanish moss to sides of can at top for hair; glue a clump under eyes for mustache.

7. *Eyeglasses:* Wrap wire around dowel to make spectacles. Trim off excess wire; cement glasses in place.

8. Tie fabric strip in a bow; glue at center bottom of can.

9. *Sign:* Glue dowel to center back of 4" wooden piece; paint both buttermilk. Write "Happy Birthday Papaw!" on wood with bluebell wood marker. ❀

"Stained Glass" Butterfly

Enjoy the color of stained glass with none of the fuss! Our fun and simple version is easy enough for kids—just create a colorful mosaic of tissue paper on a base cut from a throw-away plastic lid!

Design by Helen Rafson

"Stained Glass" Butterfly

Red, yellow, orange, and purple tissue paper

Black tissue paper

Let's Begin!

Materials

- ☐ Flat clear or translucent plastic lid from a container like a coffee can
- ☐ Tissue paper: black, red, yellow, orange and purple
- ☐ Tracing paper
- ☐ Shiny black #SC 139 Scribbles dimensional paint from Duncan Crafts
- ☐ Clear acrylic matte sealer from Plaid Enterprises
- ☐ Mod Podge from Plaid Enterprises
- ☐ Aleene's Tacky Glue
- ☐ Masking tape
- ☐ Needle
- ☐ Nylon thread
- ☐ Foam paintbrush

Project Notes

Refer to photo and pattern throughout.

Follow manufacturer's instructions for using Modge Podge.

Instructions

1. Clean and dry plastic lid; trim off side edges.

2. Trace pattern onto tracing paper. Tape pattern to plastic so pattern shows through. Trace over pattern outline and other details with black dimensional paint; let dry completely.

3. Tear tissue paper into small pieces. Apply to back (unpainted) side of butterfly with Modge Podge, filling in body and head with black tissue paper and creating a colorful mosaic of other colors on wings. Let dry.

4. Spray back of butterfly with acrylic matte sealer; let dry.

5. Carefully trim away excess plastic, cutting as close to black outline as possible. Be especially careful when trimming next to antennae, and leave a small portion of clear plastic between bases of antennae for threading through hanger. Pierce this area with a needle and thread a hanging loop of nylon thread through hole. ❀

Stenciled Rag Rug

Transform an inexpensive scatter rug from the discount store into a unique accent piece for the home. All it takes are simple painted designs and an easy sewn-on edging in a coordinating plaid fabric.

Design by Barbara Woolley

Project Notes

Refer to photo throughout.

Let paints dry between applications.

Amount of fabric needed may vary depending on the size of your rug.

Follow manufacturer's instructions for applying paints and stencils.

Instructions

1. Tear—do not cut—fabric into 1½"-wide strips.

2. Using marker, measure and mark a line 1" from each long edge of rug. Using large-eye needle threaded with fabric strips, blanket-stitch along long edges, working from marked line over edge.

Knot fabric each time you begin or end a fabric strip, and secure each knot with a drop of glue.

3. Measure and mark another line around rug 2" from edges along long sides and 1½" from edges along short sides. Using large-eye needle threaded with fabric strips, sew a running stitch around rug over marked line. Again, knot fabric when beginning or ending a fabric strip, and secure each knot with glue.

4. Add painted designs to rug as desired using stencils and selected colors of paint. ❀

Materials

- ☐ Loosely woven cotton rug
- ☐ Approximately ½ yard of woven checked or plaid fabric in complementary color
- ☐ Tulip matte dimensional paints in desired colors from Duncan Enterprises
- ☐ Tulip Stick-Ease Stencils from Duncan Enterprises: Flights of Fancy #SL003 and Snazzy Daisies #SL004
- ☐ Stencil brush or sponge
- ☐ Marvy's Erasable Fabric Marker from Uchida of America
- ☐ Craft adhesive
- ☐ Large-eye needle

Lacy Fern Bucket

Borrow a delicate design from nature to create this exquisite tote. It's great for camouflaging a less-than-lovely flowerpot, and it makes a delightful gift container, too.

Design by Barbara Woolley

Let's Begin!

Materials

- ☐ Size 5 (6½"-high and 8¼"-diameter) painter's bucket
- ☐ 4 (2") wooden ball knobs
- ☐ Fancy Fern #72109 decorative stamp from Rubber Stampede
- ☐ CeramDecor PermEnamel paints from Delta: tangerine #45008, true green #45012, maize #45014, sea foam green #45027, hunter green #45032, adobe clay #45039 and cream #45118
- ☐ Eagle Millennium paintbrush #710-20 from Eagle Brush Inc.
- ☐ Small white makeup-blending sponge
- ☐ Craft cement
- ☐ Household vinegar
- ☐ Masking tape

Project Notes

Refer to photo throughout.

Let all paints dry between applications.

Instructions

1. Wash bucket in a solution of vinegar water; as much as possible, avoid touching the areas to be painted with your bare hands. You do not want to leave any fingerprints on the bucket.

2. Using sponge, apply an even layer of cream paint to interior and exterior of bucket.

3. Measure a line 1" below top rim of bucket and mark lightly with a pencil. To obtain a clean, sharp edge, run masking tape along this line to expose an even 1" band around top of bucket. Repeat to mask a 1" band around bottom of bucket.

4. Sponge bands with adobe clay. Let dry before removing masking tape.

5. Paint rolled top edge of bucket sea foam green.

6. Using wooden end of

paintbrush handle (or eraser on a new pencil), stamp an even row of sea foam green dots around top and bottom of both adobe clay bands on outside of bucket. Stamp a row of adobe clay dots around top edge of bucket's interior.

7. Sponge or brush knobs with sea foam green. Stamp adobe clay dots randomly over surface.

8. Using sponge, apply paints to fern stamp, using a mixture of colors—including all the greens, tangerine and maize—for a natural, realistic look. Stamp ferns randomly onto bucket, inside and out.

9. Sponge or brush a thin coat of glaze over all painted surfaces of bucket and ball knobs.

10. Cement ball knobs to bottom of bucket for feet. ❀

Checkerboard Tray Table

Thrift shops and garage sales yield perfectly serviceable TV trays, often for less than a buck apiece. Give them new life with a simple painted design.

Design by Barbara Matthiessen

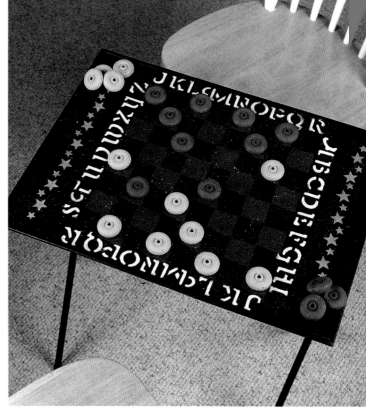

Let's Begin!

Materials
- 15" x 21" flat-top TV tray with legs
- 24 (1½") wooden toy wheels from Walnut Hollow
- Krylon products: sandable primer and crystal clear acrylic sealer
- FolkArt acrylic paints from Plaid Enterprises: wicker white #901, yellow ochre #917, calico red #932 and licorice #938
- Stencils from Plaid Enterprises: Old Tyme Block #28551 1" alphabet and star #28773
- Treasure Gold silver paste from Plaid Enterprises
- Natural jute twine
- Chalk
- Painter's tape
- 1¼" square of sponge
- Paintbrush
- Stencil brush
- Old toothbrush or spatter brush
- Medium-grit sandpaper

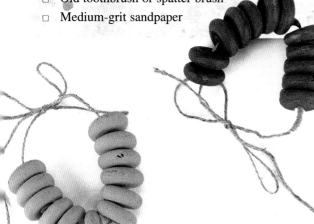

Project Notes
Refer to photo throughout.

Follow manufacturer's instructions for using primer, silver paste and sealer.

Let all coats of primer, paint and sealer dry between applications.

Instructions
1. Clean tray and legs with soap and water; allow to dry thoroughly.

2. Apply primer to all surfaces of tray and legs.

3. Paint tray and most of legs licorice, allowing some spots of rust-colored primer to show through on legs. Paint 12 wheels calico red and 12 yellow ochre.

4. Rub silver paste randomly over legs to mimic the appearance of metal showing through.

5. Using chalk, mark off a 12" square in center of tray. Apply painter's tape just outside chalked lines. Divide square into eight rows of 1½" squares.

6. Dip sponge in calico red; dab off excess paint. Sponge every other square, redipping sponge in paint after every fourth or fifth square. Remove painter's tape.

7. Position alphabet stencil along sides of checkerboard. Tape edges of stencil to hold it in place. Apply a little wicker white to stencil brush and stencil letters.

8. Using star stencil and stencil brush dipped in yellow ochre, stencil a starry border across short ends of tray.

9. Thin a nickel-size puddle of yellow ochre with enough water to yield an inky consistency. Using toothbrush or spatter brush, spatter painted tray lightly with mixture.

10. Seal painted tray and legs with two coats of sealer.

11. Sand painted wheels lightly; thread them onto strands of jute twine and tie to tray legs. ✿

Kitchen Chick Pot Holder Set

A chicken and eggs lend a warm, homey touch to ready-made kitchen pot holders. These make great shower gifts or presents to welcome a new neighbor.

Designs by Chris Malone

Project Notes

Refer to photo and patterns throughout.

Follow manufacturer's instructions for using fusible adhesive.

Use 2 strands of black embroidery floss for all embroidery.

Instructions

1. Fuse adhesive onto wrong side of fabrics with iron. Cut pattern pieces from fused fabric: beak from gold print; wing, comb and wattle from red-and-black check; body from brown print; and one egg from each of three tan and/or light brown prints or plaids.

2. Peel backing from chicken pieces and arrange on one pot holder, overlapping pieces where indicated by dashed lines. Fuse in place. Arrange eggs on second pot holder; fuse in place.

3. Using black embroidery floss, blanket-stitch around all appliqués; stitch chicken's legs and feet with stem stitch or backstitch.

4. *Sew buttons to points indicated by dots on patterns:* Sew black button to chicken's head for eye using black floss. Using tan sewing thread throughout, sew 7⁄16" mottled brown buttons below chicken; sew 5⁄8"-7⁄8" tan/light brown button to center of each egg. ❀

Let's Begin!

Materials

☐ 2 solid, checked or plaid fabric pot holders

☐ Cotton fabrics: 4½" x 3½" brown print, 2" x 3" piece of each of three tan and/or light brown prints or plaids, 2" x 3" red-and-black check and 1" square gold print

☐ HeatnBond Lite fusible adhesive from Therm O Web

☐ Black 6-strand embroidery floss

☐ Embroidery needle

☐ Tan sewing thread

☐ Flat buttons: ⅜" black, 5 (7⁄16") mottled brown and 3 (5⁄8"–7⁄8") tan/light brown

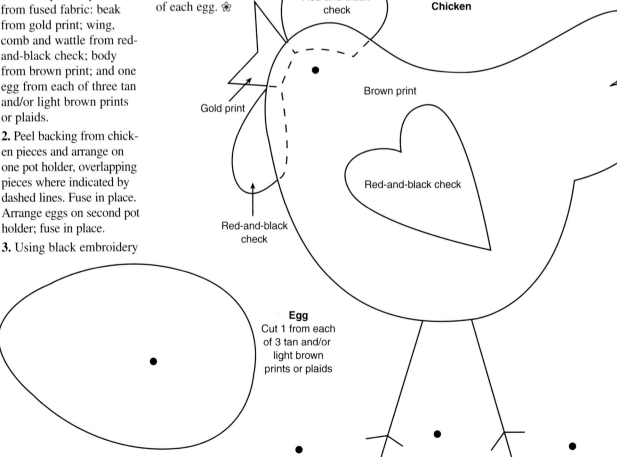

Red-and-black check

Chicken

Gold print

Brown print

Red-and-black check

Red-and-black check

Egg
Cut 1 from each of 3 tan and/or light brown prints or plaids

School Days

Celebrate the end of another successful school year, or even a graduation, with this pair of fun tin-punch projects!

Designs by Sandra Graham Smith

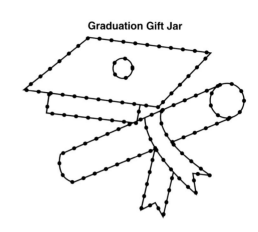

Graduation Gift Jar

Let's Begin!

Materials for Gift Jar

- ½-pint wide-mouth jar with unprinted lid
- Glossy enamel paints: black, white and red
- Small artist paintbrush
- Pressed-wood board or other hard, protective surface
- Black ultra-fine-point permanent marking pen
- Several finishing nails
- Tracing paper
- Masking tape
- Hammer

Project Notes

Refer to photo and pattern throughout.

Let all paints dry between applications.

Instructions

1. Trace pattern onto tracing paper. Cut out to fit on top of lid. Tape pattern in place.

2. Place lid on protective surface. Use hammer to tap nail from dot to dot, piercing lid. Change nail when point dulls.

3. Hold up punched lid to light; repunch any holes where necessary. Remove pattern and tape.

4. Paint designs inside punched lines using thick strokes. Paint mortarboard black, diploma white and ribbon red.

5. When dry, Write "Congratulations" and graduate's name and year on diploma.

6. Fill jar with candy, quarters, etc.

Continued on page 45

School Days Pie Tin

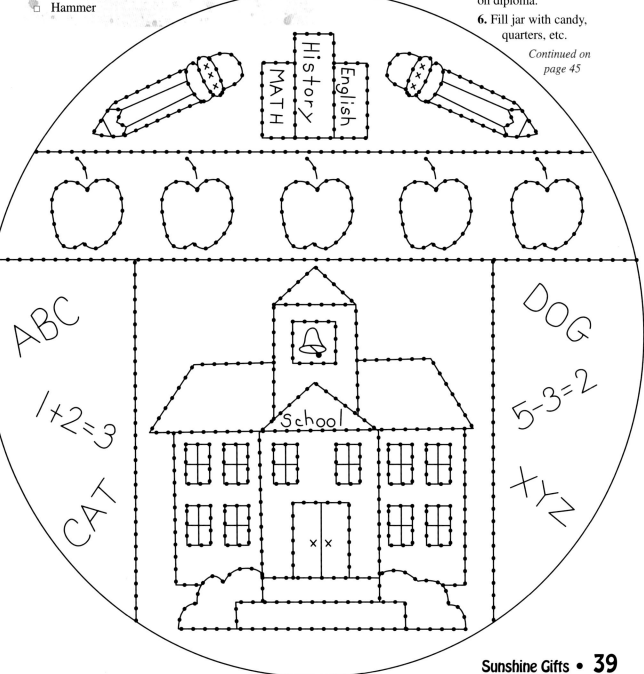

Foam Floral Basket

Change a yard-sale basket into a lovely container for guest towels, bath necessities or other odds and ends with the addition of colorful craft foam flowers.

Design by Barbara Matthiessen

Let's Begin!

Materials
- Basket
- Craft foam: 1 sheet each green, pink, purple and white and ½ sheet yellow
- ZIG Writers 1.2mm pigment ink pens from EK Success Ltd.: brown, pink, purple and green
- ZIG Millennium 0.5mm black marker from EK Success Ltd.
- Fabri-Tac Glue from Beacon Adhesives
- Small, stiff stencil brush or fabric-painting brush

Project Note
Refer to photo and patterns throughout.

Instructions
1. Trace flowers and leaves onto foam with black marker and cut out just outside traced lines: *green*—eight small leaves and four large leaves; *pink*—four small, two medium and two large flowers; *purple*—two large, two medium and two small flowers; *white*—two large, four medium and two small flowers; *yellow*—four ⅞" circles and four 1½" circles for flower centers.

2. Shade edges and centers of leaves with green pigment ink pen. Run pen along edge for a few inches, then use stiff bristle brush to spread ink toward center. In same manner, shade edges of white and pink flowers with pink pen, purple flowers with purple pen and yellow flower centers with brown pen.

3. Using black marker, outline all flowers with wiggly lines. Draw lines radiating out from centers of flowers. Draw veins on leaves. Outline flower centers with wiggly lines, then add tiny dots inside outlines.

4. Glue a large flower center to each large purple and white flower; glue a small flower center to each medium white flower.

5. Glue flowers and leaves to sides of basket and up handle. On sample each side has a large pink flower and a large purple flower, a medium white flower and a medium purple flower, two small pink flowers and a small white flower, two large leaves and two small leaves. Each side of handle, from base of handle up, includes one large white flower, small purple flower, small leaf, pink medium flower, small leaf and white medium flower. Leave center of handle free to make it easier to carry basket. ❀

Large Leaf

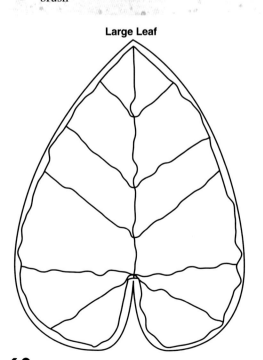

Large Flower

Small Flower

Small Leaf

Medium Flower

Star Bright Photo Frame

A simple snapshot becomes a lovely gift when it's framed in this stenciled papier-mâché frame.

Design by Mary Ayres

Let's Begin!

Materials

- 6½" square papier-mâché frame from D&CC
- 2 Woodsies ⅞" wooden stars from Forster Inc.
- Simply Stencils Moon and Stars stencil #28359 from Plaid Enterprises
- Americana acrylic paints from DecoArt: antique white #DA58 and rookwood red #DA97
- Emperor's gold #DA148 Dazzling Metallics acrylic paint from DecoArt
- Weathered Wood Crackling Medium from DecoArt
- Paintbrushes: #8 round bristle and 2 (½") stencil brushes
- ZIG fine-tip black permanent marker from EK Success Ltd.
- Masking tape
- Tacky craft glue

Project Notes

Refer to photo throughout.

Refer to directions for base-coating, dry-brushing and stenciling under "Painting Techniques" in General Instructions on page 191.

Instructions

1. Base-coat front and sides of frame with rookwood red; base-coat back of frame with antique white. Let dry.

2. Brush one coat of crackling medium on front and sides of frame. Let dry thoroughly, 20–60 minutes.

3. Brush one coat of antique white atop dry crackling medium. Cracks will form within minutes.

4. Dry-brush edges of frame with emperor's gold.

Lightly pencil border lines on frame front ¼" in from outside edge and edge of photo opening.

5. Stencil moon and stars on frame front using emperor's gold and shading edges with rookwood red.

6. Using black marker, outline stenciled moon and each star with dotted line. Apply dotted line along penciled border lines, taking care not to dot over any painted tips of stars.

7. Paint wooden stars with emperor's gold; dry-brush edges with rookwood red. When dry, use marker to draw dotted line around front edge of each. Glue stars around photo opening as shown, overlapping opening somewhat. ❀

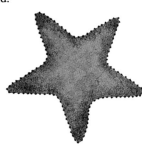

Colorful Crayon Catchall

Children will enjoy receiving and helping you make this handy desktop organizer crafted from a recycled soup or vegetable can and colorful pieces of craft foam.

Design by Helen Rafson

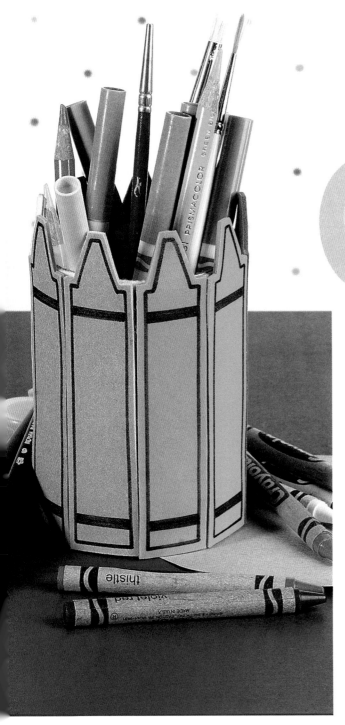

Let's Begin!

Materials

- Craft foam sheets: dark pink, orange, purple, red, yellow, lavender, pink, blue and green
- Fine-line black permanent marking pen
- 3⅞" x 8⅝" piece white felt
- Empty 10½-ounce soup can with one end removed, washed, dried, and any sharp edges filed smooth
- Tacky craft glue

Project Note

Refer to photo and pattern throughout.

Instructions

1. Cut one crayon from each of the nine colors of craft foam. Add details with fine-line black marking pen.

2. Glue felt around can to cover it; let dry. Glue crayons, edge to edge and bottoms even, around can. Let dry. ❀

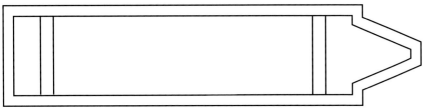

Crayon
Cut 9, 1 each from dark pink, orange, purple, red, yellow, lavender, pink, blue and green craft foam

Sunny Smile Mug & Trivet

Let a special friend face the day with a smile along with that vital cup of java! The painted mug is colorful and cheery, and the companion trivet boasts a glowing sun with a big smile.

Designs by Annie Lang

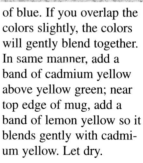

Let's Begin!

Materials

Each Project

☐ Transfer paper

☐ UltraGloss air-cure enamel paints from DecoArt: white #DG1, gloss black #DG2, lemon yellow #DG5, cadmium yellow #DG6, orange #DG7, Christmas red #DG10, true blue #DG30, purple #DG33 and yellow green #DG51

☐ Paintbrushes: #5 and #10 pointed rounds and size 1 liner

Mug

☐ White or off-white ceramic mug

☐ 1" square cut from household sponge

Trivet

☐ 4" square white ceramic tile

☐ 4" square yellow felt

☐ Craft glue

Project Notes

Refer to photo and patterns throughout.

Refer to directions for transferring pattern under "Using Transfer Paper" in General Instructions on page 191.

Refer to paint manufacturer's instructions for washing painted pieces.

Mug

1. Wash mug in soapy water; rinse well and dry thoroughly.

2. Paint mug by sponging bands of color up from base, graduating colors until you reach the rim. To sponge on color, dampen sponge and wring out until it is almost dry. Dip sponge into paint and pounce it up and down on palette a few times to work paint into the sponge. Then gently pounce color up and down on surface.

3. Starting at base, sponge a line of true blue around mug. While still a little wet, sponge a line of yellow green along top edge of blue. If you overlap the colors slightly, the colors will gently blend together. In same manner, add a band of cadmium yellow above yellow green; near top edge of mug, add a band of lemon yellow so it blends gently with cadmium yellow. Let dry.

4. Repeat sponging technique used for background, painting handle. Beginning at base of handle, sponge on purple, then Christmas red, then orange. Let dry.

5. Transfer lettering onto opposite sides of mug. Using #10 round brush, paint letters black. Using #5 brush and black, outline lettering and add "movement" lines. Let dry.

Trivet

1. Wash ceramic tile in soapy water; rinse well and dry thoroughly.

2. Transfer sun pattern to center of tile, making sure points of large sun rays rest on all four tile corners before you begin transferring.

3. Using #10 round brush, paint sun lemon yellow. When dry, use #5 brush to paint cadmium yellow outline around sunshine border and around center face area. When dry, retransfer face details as needed. Use #5 brush to tap a little orange onto cheeks. Paint nose orange. When dry, add tiny white highlight dots to each cheek and nose. Fill in mouth with black using #5 brush. Add black eyes, mouth details and outlining and squiggly detail lines with liner brush.

4. Glue felt square to bottom of trivet. ✿

Trivet

Mug

Smile!

School Days continued from page 39

Let's Begin!

Materials for Pie Tin

- ☐ 9" metal pie tin
- ☐ Glossy enamel paints: black, white, red, yellow, green, light brown, gray and pink
- ☐ Small artist paintbrush
- ☐ Pressed-wood board or other hard, protective surface
- ☐ Hammer
- ☐ Several finishing nails
- ☐ Tracing paper
- ☐ Masking tape
- ☐ Black ultra-fine-point permanent marking pen
- ☐ Marvy's white extra-fine opaque marker from Uchida
- ☐ 12" piece (⅛"-wide) red satin ribbon

Project Notes

Refer to photo and pattern (pages 38 and 39) throughout.

Let all paints dry between applications.

Instructions

1. Trace pattern onto tracing paper. Cut out to fit in bottom of pie tin. Tape pattern in place.

2. Place tin on protective surface. Use hammer to tap nail from dot to dot, piercing tin. Change nail when point dulls.

3. Hold up punched tin to light; repunch any holes where necessary. Remove pattern and tape.

4. Paint designs inside punched lines using thick strokes: *black*—center top and side roofs, doors, side panels, pencil points and bands below pencil erasers; *white*—all windows in school and rim of pie tin; *red*—apples and walls of schoolhouse; *yellow*—middle book and barrels of pencils; *green*—"bushes" beside steps and leaves to right of apple stems; *light brown*—pencil erasers and "wood" near points of pencils; *gray*—steps, triangular roof section over door;

bands above yellow portions of pencils; and left-hand book; *pink*—right-hand book.

5. Paint yellow bell in bell-tower window.

6. Using fine-point black marker, add words on books, lines on pencils and windows, "School" over doors and outline of bell. Add wording around rim of pie tin.

7. Using white marker. Add dots on black bands on pencil; add doorknobs and line down center of school doors; add words and sums to side "blackboard" sections.

8. Thread ribbon through two holes in top center of tin; tie ends to make hanging loop. ❧

"You Make My Heart Soar"

Combine simple, stuffed felt shapes with a heartfelt sentiment to make a lovely thank-you gift or a permanent reminder of just how special someone is to you.

Design by Chris Malone

Let's Begin!

Materials

- □ Rainbow Felt Classic from Kunin Mfg.: 1 sheet each red #064 and gold #352 and 2 sheets white #550
- □ Black 6-strand embroidery floss
- □ Embroidery needle
- □ Polyester fiberfill
- □ Flat black buttons: 2 (1"); 2 (½") and 1 (⅝")
- □ Tracing paper
- □ 48" piece (19-gauge) black craft wire
- □ Dowel, pencil or spoon handle
- □ Craft glue or hot-glue gun and glue sticks

Project Notes

Refer to photo and patterns, below and on page 48, throughout.

Use 2 strands of black embroidery floss for all stitching.

Instructions

1. Cut two hearts from red felt, two large stars and four small stars from gold felt, and two wings from white felt, placing dashed line along fold.

2. Trace lettering onto tracing paper; pin or baste to center of one heart. Stitching through paper and felt, backstitch lettering. When completed, gently tug paper away from felt. Add French knots at ends of letters where indicated by dots.

3. Pin hearts together with stitched side on top. Blanket-stitch together around edges, stuffing lightly with fiberfill as you stitch.

4. Pin wings together. Blanket-stitch together around edges and sew a running stitch down center of wings. Apply glue along running stitch on one side; press to center back of heart.

5. Pin stars together in pairs; sew together with running stitch, stitching about ⅛" from edge. Sew ½" button in center of each smaller star; sew ⅝" button in center of larger star.

6. Sew 1" buttons to top "lobes" of heart. Wrap one end of wire around button about 6" from tip of wire. Curl 6" length by wrapping it around dowel. Push curls down onto heart so sharp tip of wire is not exposed. Curl remaining length of wire gently around dowel; shape into hanger. Wrap and curl remaining end around other button.

7. Glue smaller stars to heart; glue larger heart to wire hanger. ❁

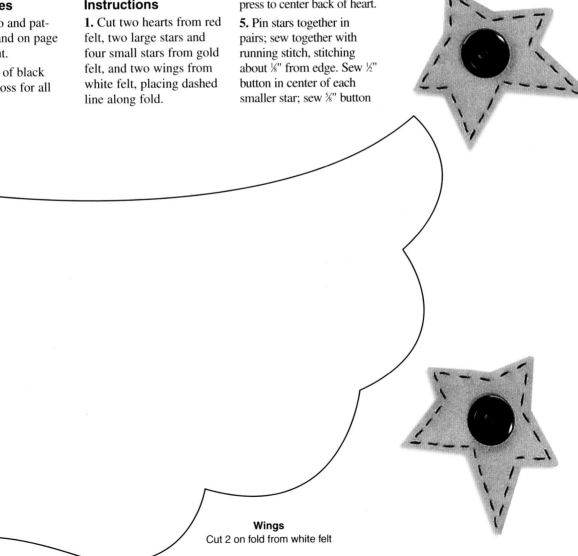

Place on fold

Wings
Cut 2 on fold from white felt

You make my heart Soar

Small Star
Cut 4 from gold felt

Large Star
Cut 2 from gold felt

Heart
Cut 2 from red felt

Friendly Flower Note Cards

Here's a great way to use up those scraps of decorative paper you accumulate for your scrapbook projects. Gift-wrap remnants work fine, too.

Design by Mary Ayres

Friendly Flower Note Cards

Let's Begin!

Materials
Both Note Cards

- 2 (4¼" x 5½") white note cards with matching envelopes
- Assorted print and solid decorative papers from The Paper Patch: turquoise, pink, orange, blue, purple, yellow and green
- ZIG twin-tip black permanent marker from EK Success Ltd.
- Round paper punches from Fiskars: ⁵⁄₁₆" and ¼"
- Glue stick

Project Note
Refer to photo and pattern throughout.

Instructions
1. For background squares as shown on pattern, cut two 3¾" x 5" rectangles from turquoise paper. Cut petals, one each from orange and pink (do not cut out center). Cut edging around face, one each from blue and purple (do not cut out center). Cut two faces from yellow. For each, cut leaf and stem in one piece from green.

2. From pink paper, punch two ⁵⁄₁₆" circles for cheeks and one ¼" circle for nose for each card.

3. Using fine tip of marker, draw "stitching lines" and "blanket stitch" on all pieces as shown.

4. Glue turquoise rectangle to center of each card. Glue on stem and leaves, petals, edging for face, yellow face, cheeks and nose. Add dashed smile with fine tip of marker; dot on eyes using side of marker's bullet tip. ❀

Tin Can May "Baskets"

Recycle a tin can and add decorations of craft foam to make a delightful little tote to fill with flowers or treats.

Design by Chris Malone

Let's Begin!

Materials
Each Basket

- ☐ Empty tin can with one end removed, washed, dried, and any sharp edges filed smooth
- ☐ Craft foam sheets: white, pink, black, yellow and green, plus scraps of other assorted colors as desired
- ☐ Shiny black dimensional paint
- ☐ Black fine-line permanent marking pen
- ☐ 52" piece (19-gauge) black craft wire
- ☐ 1½" x 15" strip torn fabric in a coordinating pastel
- ☐ Fabri-Tac permanent adhesive from Beacon Adhesives
- ☐ Wire cutters
- ☐ ¼"- and ½"-diameter wooden dowels or spoon handles
- ☐ Hammer and large nail

Project Note
Refer to photo and patterns throughout.

Bee Basket
1. Using hammer and nail, punch two holes opposite each other near top (open) edge of can for attaching handle later. Smooth any rough edges.

2. Measure can. To cover, cut a strip of pink foam as wide as the can is tall and as long as the can's diameter plus ½". Glue to can, overlapping edges in back.

3. Cut two ½"-wide strips of black foam the same length as pink piece; glue one at top edge and one at bottom, overlapping ends in back.

4. Cut three petal flowers from white foam, three leaves from green and three small circles for flower centers from yellow. Glue to front of can as shown. Add dots to flower centers with black dimensional paint; outline centers, leaves and flowers with marking pen.

5. Cut one bee body from yellow foam, two wings from white, and two stripes to fit bee's body from black. Glue stripes atop body; glue wings to wrong side of bee's body. Outline wings with marking pen; add eye to bee with black dimensional paint.

6. Cut wire into a 40" and a 12" length. Insert one end of 40" piece through hole in can, poking wire through foam. Push wire end 6" into can and twist several times to hold it in place. Wrap wire randomly around large dowel to curl it; push remaining end through hole on other side of can and twist to secure. Curl 6" ends on either side with smaller dowel.

Arrange curls so sharp tips of wire are not exposed.

7. Curl 12" piece of wire around smaller dowel. Glue one end to back of bee; twist other end around wire handle. Tie fabric strip around handle in a bow.

Butterfly Basket
1. Repeat steps 1–3 as for bee basket, covering can with white foam instead of pink.

2. Cut one petal flower each from red and blue foam; cut one round flower from purple foam; cut three leaves from green; and cut smaller circles for flower centers, one each from yellow, pink and orange. Glue to front of can as shown. Add dots to flower centers with black dimensional paint; outline centers, leaves and flowers with marking pen.

3. Cut one butterfly body from black foam, one set of wings from blue, and two small circles each from pink and purple. Glue circles and body to wings. Outline wings with marking pen; add eyes with black dimensional paint.

4. Repeat steps 6 and 7 as for bee basket, gluing butterfly to handle. ✿

Bee Wing
Cut 2 from white craft foam

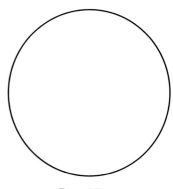

Round Flower
Cut 1 from purple craft foam

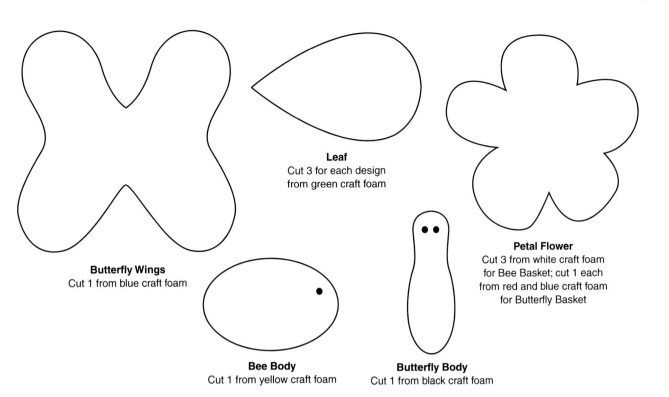

Leaf
Cut 3 for each design
from green craft foam

Petal Flower
Cut 3 from white craft foam
for Bee Basket; cut 1 each
from red and blue craft foam
for Butterfly Basket

Butterfly Wings
Cut 1 from blue craft foam

Bee Body
Cut 1 from yellow craft foam

Butterfly Body
Cut 1 from black craft foam

Craft It, Wear It!

With just a dab of paint, a sprinkling of beads and a stitch here and there, your old vests, sweatshirts and T-shirts can take on a gorgeous new life! Jump into this chapter and discover the cute designs for women and kids at your fingertips!

Frogs & Butterflies Sweatshirt

A whimsical design transforms a plain white sweatshirt into a colorful cardigan-style topper.

Design by Mary Ayres

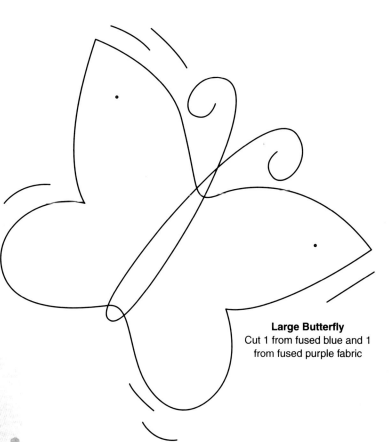

Large Butterfly
Cut 1 from fused blue and 1 from fused purple fabric

Let's Begin!

Materials

- Women's white sweatshirt
- Print or solid cotton fabrics: ¼ yard green, ⅛ yard yellow, and scraps of purple, blue, pink and orange
- Flat buttons: 2 (⅞₆") gray, 2 (⅞₆") yellow, 2 (⅝₆") pink and 2 (⅝₆") blue
- Cotton embroidery floss to match fabrics: brown, green, yellow, orange, blue, pink and purple
- Sewing threads: white and yellow
- Embroidery needle and hand-sewing needle
- HeatnBond Ultra Hold iron-on adhesive from Therm O Web
- Iron

Project Notes

Refer to photo and patterns (page 54–56) throughout.

Use 3 strands of embroidery floss for all embroidery; wrap floss around needle three times for each French knot.

Follow manufacturer's instructions for using iron-on adhesive.

Instructions

1. Cut sweatshirt straight down center from neck through waistband. From yellow fabric, cut two 2"-wide strips long enough to bind cut edges; strips should be 1" longer than edge.

2. With wrong side of fabric facing right side of sweatshirt, pin strips to front edges of sweatshirt with edges even and ends of binding strips extending ½" past neck and bottom of sweatshirt. Sew strips to sweatshirt ½" from edges. Turn ends of strips under so they are even with sweatshirt. Turn long raw edges of strips under ½", then fold strips over cut edge of sweatshirt fabric to back; pin to hold. Sew turned edges of strips to back of sweatshirt using an invisible stitch and yellow thread.

3. Fuse adhesive to wrong side of yellow, pink, purple, green, orange and blue fabrics. Cut two frogs, reversing one, from green fused fabric; two nets, reversing one, from yellow; small butterfly from pink and another from orange, and large butterfly from purple and another from blue.

4. Peel backing from appliqué pieces; fuse frog, net, pink and purple butterflies to left side of vest, and remaining pieces to right side.

5. Using floss to match fabrics, add embroidered details:

Frogs—With green, embroider buttonhole stitch around frogs, including hands that hold nets, and French knot nostrils; add three yellow French knots to cheeks; add brown French knot eyes and add mouths with stem stitch.

Nets—Using brown stem stitch throughout, outline nets; add netting pattern over yellow fabric, net handles, and "motion lines."

Butterflies—Using brown stem stitch throughout, fill in butterfly bodies, sewing around and around until shape is filled; add antennae and "motion lines." Using embroidery floss to match fabric, sew buttonhole stitch around each butterfly.

6. Using white sewing thread, sew pairs of buttons in butterflies' upper wings: yellow buttons on pink butterflies, blue buttons on purple butterflies, pink buttons on blue butterflies and gray buttons on orange butterflies. ❀

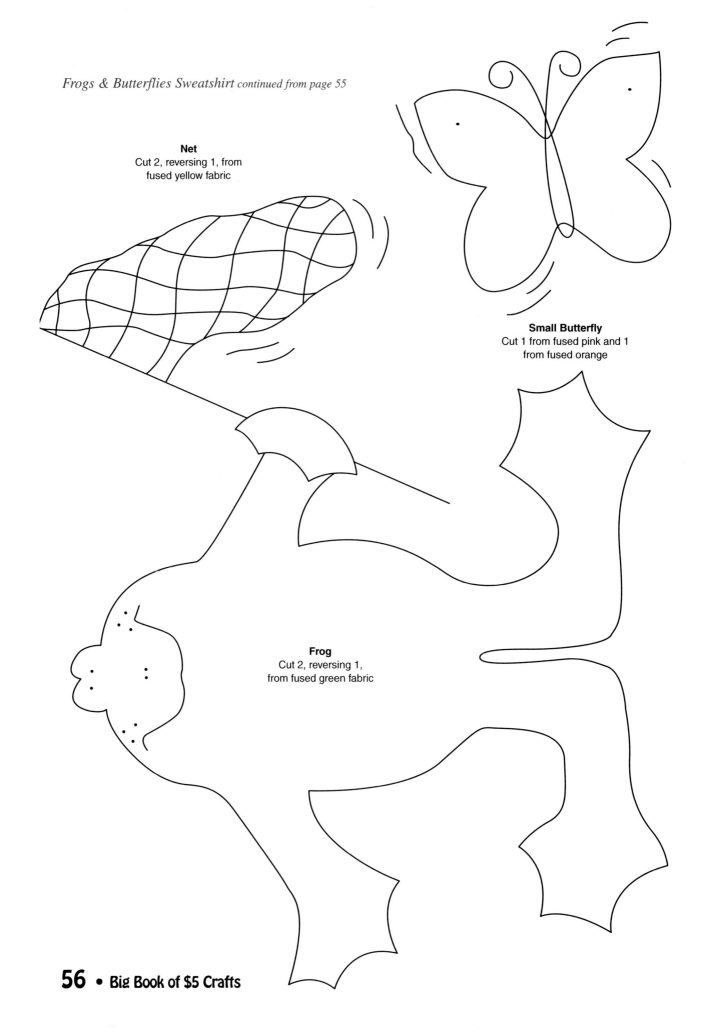

Net
Cut 2, reversing 1, from
fused yellow fabric

Small Butterfly
Cut 1 from fused pink and 1
from fused orange

Frog
Cut 2, reversing 1,
from fused green fabric

Heart's Delight Sweatshirt

This cozy sweatshirt boasts lots of country-style charm thanks to heart-shaped doilies enhanced with calico prints and buttons.

Design by Mary Ayres

Let's Begin!

Materials

- Rose sweatshirt
- 3 (3") heart-shaped white cutwork doilies from Wimpole Street Creations
- Scraps of calico print fabrics: purple, rose and blue
- 3 (⅝") flat rose-colored buttons
- Cotton embroidery floss: burgundy and pink
- Embroidery needle
- HeatnBond Ultra Hold iron-on adhesive from Therm O Web
- Iron

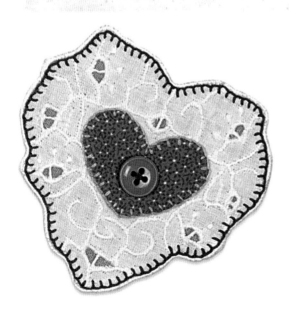

Project Notes

Refer to photo throughout.

Follow manufacturer's instructions for using iron-on adhesive.

Instructions

1. Pin heart doilies across center top of sweatshirt. Using 3 strands burgundy floss, embroider blanket stitch stitch around each heart inside satin-stitched edge.

2. Fuse adhesive to wrong side of purple, rose and blue fabrics; cut a simple heart shape, 2" wide x 1½" high, from each piece of fabric.

3. Peel paper backing from hearts; fuse one to center of each heart, fusing purple to left-hand heart, rose to center heart and blue to right-hand heart. Embroider buttonhole stitch around each heart with 3 strands pink floss.

4. Using burgundy floss, sew button in center of each heart. ✿

Daisies Tote

Bold, bright colors give this tote contemporary flair.

Design by June Fiechter

Let's Begin!

Materials

- ☐ Large white tote bag #TB141604 from Innovo Inc.
- ☐ Ceramcoat acrylic paints from Delta: bittersweet orange #2041, leaf green #2067, white #2505, black #2506, opaque yellow #2509, pine green #2526, blue lagoon #2528 and magenta #2559
- ☐ Shiny black dimensional paint
- ☐ Crafter's paintbrushes including liner
- ☐ Delta textile medium
- ☐ Graphite paper

Project Notes

Refer to photo and pattern throughout.

Use photocopier with enlarging capabilities to enlarge pattern to 125 percent before transferring design.

Refer to directions for using transfer paper under "Transferring Designs" in General Instructions on page 190.

Follow manufacturer's instructions for mixing textile medium with paints, and mix medium with each color before painting.

Let paints dry between applications of adjacent colors.

Instructions

1. Transfer design onto center of one side of tote.

2. Paint left background square magenta, center square leaf green and right-hand square blue lagoon.

3. Paint centers of flowers opaque yellow; shade with bittersweet orange. Paint butterfly wings bittersweet orange; highlight with opaque yellow.

4. Paint stems and leaves pine green; highlight with white.

5. Using shiny black dimensional paint, add butterfly heads and bodies. Add lettering.

6. Using black acrylic paint and liner brush, add a cluster of three to five tiny highlight dots over bittersweet orange shading on one edge of each flower center; add butterfly antennae. Using tip of wooden paintbrush handle dipped in blue lagoon, dot i's in words. ❀

Enlarge design 125%
before reproducing

Fun Fish Hat

Why worry about the one that got away when a whole string of beauties splash across the crown of this cap? A little paint and ready-made buttons are all you need.

Design by June Fiechter

Let's Begin!

Materials

- Pale yellow canvas baseball cap
- 5 trout buttons #80–5B from Crafty Productions
- Delta textile medium
- Delta acrylic paints: white #2505 and Caribbean blue #2530
- ¼" fabric paint brush
- Fabric glue

Project Note

Refer to photo throughout.

Instructions

1. Referring to manufacturer's directions, mix textile medium with paints. Paint Caribbean blue waves across front of crown; paint a checkerboard pattern of white and Caribbean blue around brim about ¾" in from edge. Paint button in top of cap with Caribbean blue.

2. Glue fish buttons over waves.

3. Brush fabric glue over waves to add highlights and shine. ✿

Cool Coils Bracelet

Easy to make and fun to wear, this bracelet adds a snap of color and glitz to your ensemble.

Design by Nancy Marshall

Let's Begin!

Materials

- Beadalon Stainless Steel Remembrance bracelet-size Memory Wire
- Beadalon Colour Craft 26-gauge wire: magenta and purple
- Coiling Gizmo small rod or other ¹⁄₁₆"-diameter metal rod or skewer
- Silver-washed mushroom beads from The Beadery: 2 (9mm x 8mm) and 10 (7mm x 6mm)
- Wire cutters
- Nail clippers
- Needle-nose pliers

Project Notes

Refer to photo throughout.

Adjust size of bracelet as desired by using shorter or longer piece of Memory Wire and adjusting number of mushroom beads.

Instructions

1. Make six magenta and five purple wire-coil beads by wrapping wire around metal rod until a ¾"-long coil is made. This wire is most easily cut with a nail clippers.

2. Using wire cutters, cut 2 coils (about 18") of bracelet wire. With pliers, twist a small circle in one end to keep beads on wire.

3. Thread one of the larger mushroom beads onto bracelet wire. Slide on magenta coil, small mushroom bead, purple coil and small mushroom bead. Continue pattern until coils and beads are used, ending with magenta coil and the other larger mushroom bead. Twist circle in end of wire with needle-nose pliers, trimming off excess wire as needed. ✿

Hearts & Flowers T-Shirt

With the help of fabric yo-yos and ready-made doilies, you can make this cute T-shirt in 3 hours!

Design by Mary Ayres

Let's Begin!

Materials

- ☐ Women's V-neck T-shirt
- ☐ Scraps of 3 coordinating cotton fabrics
- ☐ 3 (2") round Battenburg doilies with fabric centers
- ☐ 6 (2") heart-shaped Battenburg doilies
- ☐ Coordinating cotton embroidery floss and embroidery needle
- ☐ White sewing thread and hand-sewing needle
- ☐ 3 (¾") coordinating flat buttons

Project Note

Refer to photo throughout.

Instructions

1. *Yo-yos:* Cut 5½" circle from each of three fabrics. Turn under raw edges ⅛"; sew running stitch close to edge all around, gathering slightly as you sew with needle and white thread. Pull thread tightly to gather; knot ends and clip. Repeat with all circles to make three yo-yos.

2. Position yo-yos evenly around neck edge, placing heart doily symmetrically on each side of each yo-yo; points of hearts should touch yo-yos and lobes of hearts should just touch each other. When placement is satisfactory, pin yo-yos and doilies in place.

3. Using an invisible stitch, sew yo-yos and hearts to T-shirt with white thread.

4. Pin round doily to center of each yo-yo. Blanket stitch around fabric center of doily using 3 strands coordinating floss.

5. Sew button to center of each round doily with 3 strands floss. ❀

Denim Sweetheart Shirt

Heart-shaped buttons look like candy hearts on the front of this painted, eyelet-trimmed shirt.

Design by Judy Atwell

Let's Begin!

Materials
- Girl's long-sleeved denim shirt
- 2 yards (2½"-wide) pregathered white eyelet trim
- Small heart-shaped buttons: 3 pink and 3 white
- Pink fabric paint
- Small heart stamp
- ½" flat soft paintbrush
- White sewing thread and hand-sewing needle
- Rotary cutter, cutting mat and straight edge
- Plastic garbage bag
- Sewing machine with zigzag stitch
- Straight pins

Project Note
Refer to photo throughout.

Instructions

1. Wash and dry shirt without using fabric softener. Iron as needed to remove wrinkles.

2. Arrange shirt on cutting mat so that all arm seams and side seams match up to horizontal lines on mat. Using rotary cutter and straight edge, cut across entire bottom of shirt, starting at highest point of hem to remove curved edges and make a straight edge to work with.

3. Match up arms seams and cuff and lay sleeves together on mat. Using rotary cutter and straight edge, cut off cuffs and shorten sleeves.

4. Thread sewing machine with white thread and set it for a close zigzag stitch. Stitch across entire bottom of shirt and both sleeve edges to finish edges before applying lace.

5. Set machine for straight stitch. Fold under about ½" of lace edge and stitch. Pin lace around bottom edge of shirt with top wrong side of lace against the lower right side edge of shirt so that overlap is about ⅜". Trim and turn under ½" on opposite edge of lace and pin in place. Starting with lace edge that already has end stitched under, stitch bottom edge of shirt; pivot at end of lace and sew down lace edge to hold in place.

6. Stitch lace around each armhole and overlap at underarm seams. Lap folded edge of lace over the first and stitch down lace to edge.

7. Remove existing buttons from shirt. Lay shirt flat on work surface. Place plastic garbage bag inside shirt to keep paint from seeping through.

8. Apply paint to heart stamp with flat brush; test it on a scrap of fabric a few times. Then stamp heart pattern over lower half of each front; let dry.

9. Turn shirt over, leaving plastic bag inside. Paint and stamp entire bottom half of shirt on back. Let dry.

10. Sew on heart buttons alternating white and pink. ❀

Denim & Lace Vest

Dress up a denim castoff with lace and ribbon roses for a quick, casual wardrobe pick-me-up.

Design by Bev Shenefield

Let's Begin!

Materials

- ☐ Denim vest with front pockets
- ☐ 1"-wide white lace with scalloped edges on both sides
- ☐ 10 blue ribbon roses with ribbon-loop leaves from C.M. Offray
- ☐ Washable fabric glue

Project Notes

Refer to photo throughout.

Number of rosettes needed may vary with size and style of your denim vest.

Transform the look of your garment by your choice of lace and ribbon roses. Consider ecru lace and/or colored lace, lace interwoven with ribbon, ribbon rosettes of different sizes and colors, and/or the addition of vintage buttons or brass charms.

Instructions

1. Raise pocket flaps. Cut lace to fit down front of vest on each side, from vest button to bottom of vest. Apply dabs of glue to back of lace; position on vest front and press in place with fingers. Close pockets.

2. Cut lace to fit around outer edge of collar. Apply glue to the back of a small section of lace; place on collar just at edge of stitching and, starting on one front edge, press lace into place with fingers, Repeat, applying glue to one small section at a time, to glue lace all around collar.

3. Starting about 1" below pocket flap, glue four ribbon rosettes down each front lace strip, spacing them evenly. Glue a rose over the lace on each point of the collar. ❀

Appliquéd Garden Shirt

Check thrift stores for a bargain shirt; add additional appliqués or some extra embroidery to cover spots, stains or small tears.

Design by Chris Malone

Let's Begin!

Materials

- ☐ Denim shirt
- ☐ Assorted fabric scraps for appliqués: red, blue pink, green, gold, black, brown and white prints and/or solids
- ☐ 6-strand cotton embroidery floss: black, red, blue, gold, green and pink
- ☐ Embroidery needle and hoop (optional)
- ☐ Iron-on adhesive
- ☐ Iron
- ☐ Cardboard cut to fit inside shirt pocket

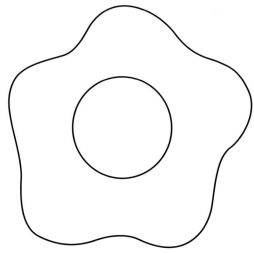

Flower A
Cut 1 flower from fused
pink and 1 center from
fused gold fabric

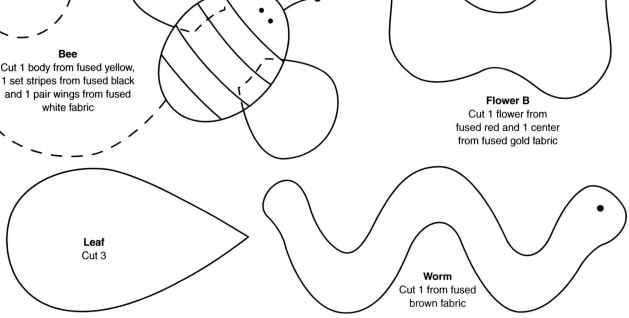

Bee
Cut 1 body from fused yellow,
1 set stripes from fused black
and 1 pair wings from fused
white fabric

Flower B
Cut 1 flower from
fused red and 1 center
from fused gold fabric

Leaf
Cut 3

Worm
Cut 1 from fused
brown fabric

Instructions

1. Fuse iron-on adhesive to backs of appliqué fabrics. Cut one flower A from pink and center from gold; one flower B from red and center from gold; one flower C from blue and center from gold; three leaves from assorted greens; one worm from brown; one bee from yellow; two bee stripes from black; two bee wings from white; two ladybug bodies from red; two ladybug heads from black, one flying bug body and head from assorted blues and two wings from gold.

2. Arrange appliqués on shirt as desired. On sample, ladybugs "walk" across top of left-hand pocket as winged bug "flies" above them. Flowers and leaves are arranged in a cluster over right-hand pocket; bee "buzzes" on right-hand pocket and worm is fused to left-hand cuff. Slip cardboard in pocket before fusing bee in place.

3. *Embroidery:* Using black floss throughout, blanket stitch around all appliqués. Add stem-stitch antennae and legs to flying bug and ladybugs; add French knot to end of each antenna and for eyes on flying bug. Add stem-stitch antennae with French knot ends to bumblebee; add French Knot eyes and running-stitch "flight path," stitching through outer layer of pocket only. Add single French knot eye to worm.

4. *Collar trim:* Measure length of collar edge; divide measurement by five (or number of floss colors desired). Using 4 strands floss, blanket stitch that length; knot and clip floss. Resume with next color. Repeat till collar is blanket-stitched all around. ❀

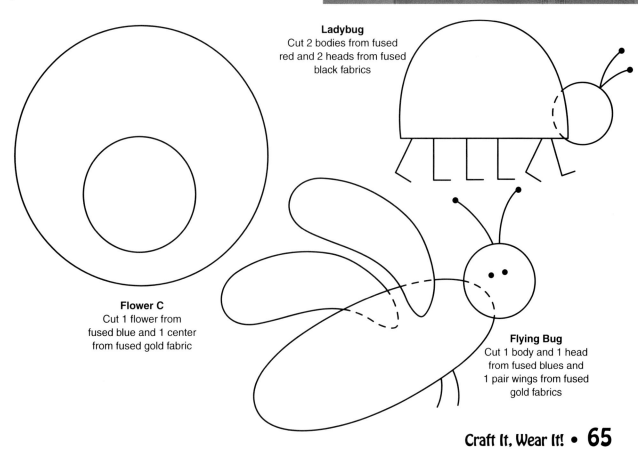

Ladybug
Cut 2 bodies from fused red and 2 heads from fused black fabrics

Flower C
Cut 1 flower from fused blue and 1 center from fused gold fabric

Flying Bug
Cut 1 body and 1 head from fused blues and 1 pair wings from fused gold fabrics

Prairie Points Tote

Simple folds of fabric in bright colors are used to create happy flowers and a vibrant edging for a simple white tote bag, transforming it into a country-style classic.

Design by Nancy Billetdeaux

Let's Begin!

Materials

- 10" x 13" x 3" white canvas tote #1992 from innovo
- Coordinating cotton fabrics: ¼ yard each red and blue and ⅛ yard green calico prints, and 5" x 13" piece gold solid
- Matching red, blue and green sewing threads and hand-sewing needle
- 3 (½") white flat buttons
- 1 yard single fold white bias tape
- Sewing machine with zigzag stitch
- Iron
- Rotary cutter and self-healing mat (optional)

Project Note

Refer to photo and Figs. 1–4 throughout.

Instructions

1. *Prairie points:* Cut 17 (3") squares red print fabric, 25 (3") squares blue print, and eight (4") squares green print. Fold each square in half with fold at top and raw edges even at bottom, wrong sides facing (Fig. 1); press. Fold top corners down to center (Fig. 2); press. Repeat with all fabric squares.

2. *Prairie point edging:* Alternating red and blue fabric triangles, lay them side by side (Fig. 3), overlapping right side of blue on top of left side of red to center of next prairie point; machine-stitch together ⅛" from raw edges to make a chain of nine red and nine blue prairie points.

3. Unfold one edge of bias tape with right side of tape lined up with raw edges of prairie points along fold line of bias tape. Fold remaining tape to other side of points and stitch again along long edge. Starting at side seam of tote bag, using large zigzag stitch and white thread, stitch prairie points to outside of bag 1" from upper edge of bag.

4. *Leaves and flower petals:* Bring one point of a green prairie point across center (Fig. 4), then bring other point across center. Repeat with remaining blue, green and red prairie points.

Fig. 1

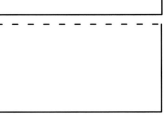

5. Lay out leaves and flowers on front of bag. Lay down green leaves first, then four flower petals with points at 12, 3, 6 and 9 o'clock positions, machine-sewing raw ends of points to bag as you go with satin stitch. Top first layer of petals with a second layer with points between those of first layer; machine-stitch raw ends in place.

6. Cut three (4") circles from gold fabric. Fold edges under ⅛" and, with needle and thread, sew gathering stitch around edge of circle. Pull thread ends tight and knot; flatten yo-yos and sew one over center of each flower. Sew white button to center of each yo-yo with yellow thread. ❀

Fig. 2

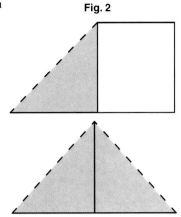

Fig. 4

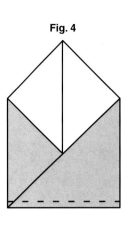

Fig. 3

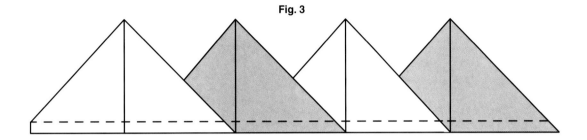

Button Brooch

Check your button jar for special metal specimens to make this classy accessory. Don't hesitate to mix silver and gold with other metal tones—the effect is lavish!

Design by Judy Atwell

Let's Begin!

Materials

- Round plastic lens from an old pair of eye glasses
- Round metal pin back
- Assortment of fancy silver and gold buttons
- A few silver and gold beads
- Wire cutters
- Tacky glue
- Small metal file

Project Notes

Refer to photo throughout.

Eleven buttons and four beads were used to make the sample.

Instructions

1. Snap shanks off backs of buttons as needed; smooth backs with metal file if necessary.

2. Glue largest button to base first. Continue gluing on smaller buttons to achieve pleasing design.

3. Cover button holes as needed by gluing on metal beads.

4. Set pin aside to dry until glue turns clear. Then glue pin back to back of pin slightly above center. ❀

Happy Birds Shirt

You can't help but smile when you wear this colorful design graced with a whole flock of vibrant birds in a rainbow of colors!

Design by Angie Wilhite

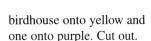

Let's Begin!

Materials

- ☐ Adult's denim shirt
- ☐ Fabric scraps in coordinating bright solids or prints: purple, yellow, lime green, raspberry, turquoise blue, tangerine
- ☐ All-purpose sewing threads to match fabrics and buttons
- ☐ Rayon embroidery threads to match fabrics
- ☐ Buttons: 22 (⅛") black round flat buttons, ½" flat round turquoise button and ½" flat round neon orange button
- ☐ Pellon products from Plaid: 1 yard Wonder-Under fusible transfer web, ⅓ yard Sof-Shape fusible interfacing, ⅛ yard Fusible Fleece, and 1⅓ yards Stitch-n-Tear fabric stabilizer
- ☐ Sewing machine with satin stitch attachment
- ☐ Iron

Project Notes

Refer to photo and patterns (pages 70–71) throughout.

Follow manufacturer's instructions for using fusible products.

Instructions

1. Wash and dry shirt and fabrics without using fabric softener; press as needed to remove wrinkles.

2. Referring to patterns for birdhouse and roof, fuse fleece to wrong side of enough raspberry, lime green, yellow and purple fabrics to make birdhouses and roofs. Fuse interfacing to back of all light-colored appliqué fabrics. Apply fusible transfer web to wrong side of all fabrics.

3. Trace shapes onto paper sides of fused fabrics that include a layer of fleece: Trace one roof onto raspberry pink and one onto lime green; trace one birdhouse onto yellow and one onto purple. Cut out.

4. Trace remaining shapes onto paper sides of fused fabrics that do not include fleece:

Small birds: Trace two bodies with wings onto tangerine with beaks from lime; trace one body with wings from purple with beak from yellow.

Medium birds: Trace two bodies with wings onto raspberry with beaks from yellow; trace three bodies with wings onto yellow with two beaks from raspberry and one from turquoise; trace one body with wings onto tangerine with beak from lime green.

Large birds: Trace one large body with wings onto turquoise with beak from tangerine, and one body with wings onto lime green with beak from purple.

Posts: Trace one each onto lime green and raspberry. Cut out.

5. Remove paper backing; arrange pieces as shown and fuse in place:

Back yoke: Medium raspberry bird with yellow beak on left side; medium yellow bird with raspberry beak and small tangerine bird with lime green beak overlapping on right.

Front left: Yellow house with raspberry roof on lime post (left) and purple house with lime roof on raspberry post (right); in front of posts, position large turquoise bird with tangerine beak and medium yellow bird with turquoise beak. Above birdhouses, place small tangerine bird with lime beak.

Front right: Above pocket, position medium yellow bird with raspberry beak and small purple bird with yellow beak. Below pocket, arrange large lime bird with purple beak, medium tangerine bird with lime beak and small raspberry bird with yellow beak.

6. Pin or baste stabilizer inside shirt to cover design areas. Using colors to match fabrics, thread sewing machine with rayon thread in top and all-purpose thread in bobbin. Satin-stitch around all elements of designs beginning with those that appear to be in back (bottom layer) and working toward front. Remove fabric stabilizer; trim threads.

7. Using threads to match buttons, sew two ⅛" buttons to each bird for eyes, orange button to purple birdhouse and turquoise button to yellow birdhouse. ✿

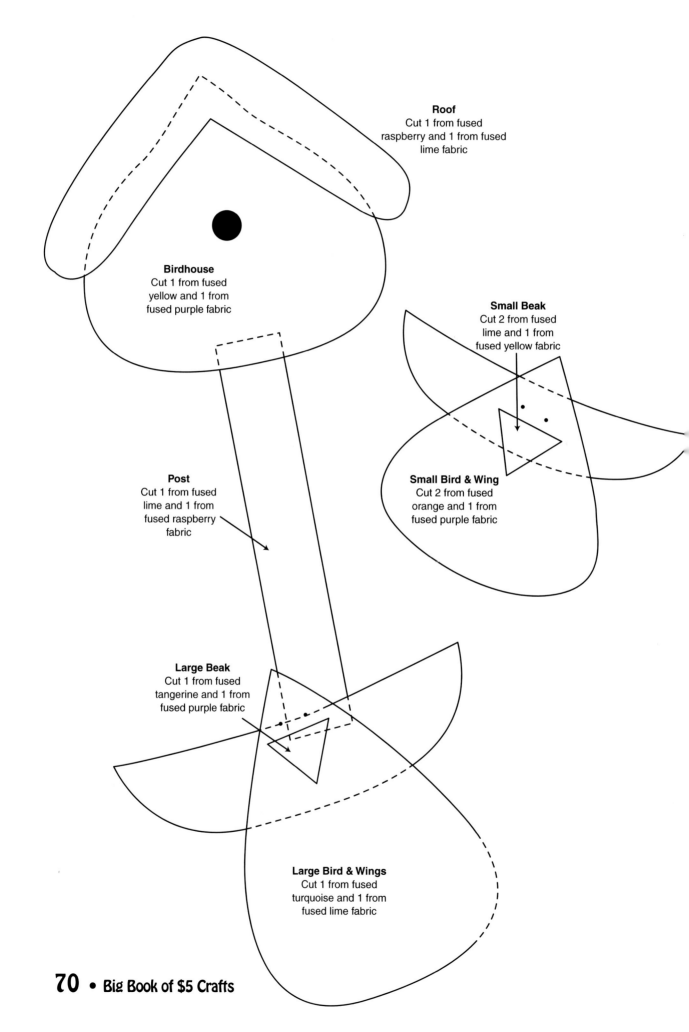

Roof
Cut 1 from fused
raspberry and 1 from fused
lime fabric

Birdhouse
Cut 1 from fused
yellow and 1 from
fused purple fabric

Small Beak
Cut 2 from fused
lime and 1 from
fused yellow fabric

Small Bird & Wing
Cut 2 from fused
orange and 1 from
fused purple fabric

Post
Cut 1 from fused
lime and 1 from
fused raspberry
fabric

Large Beak
Cut 1 from fused
tangerine and 1 from
fused purple fabric

Large Bird & Wings
Cut 1 from fused
turquoise and 1 from
fused lime fabric

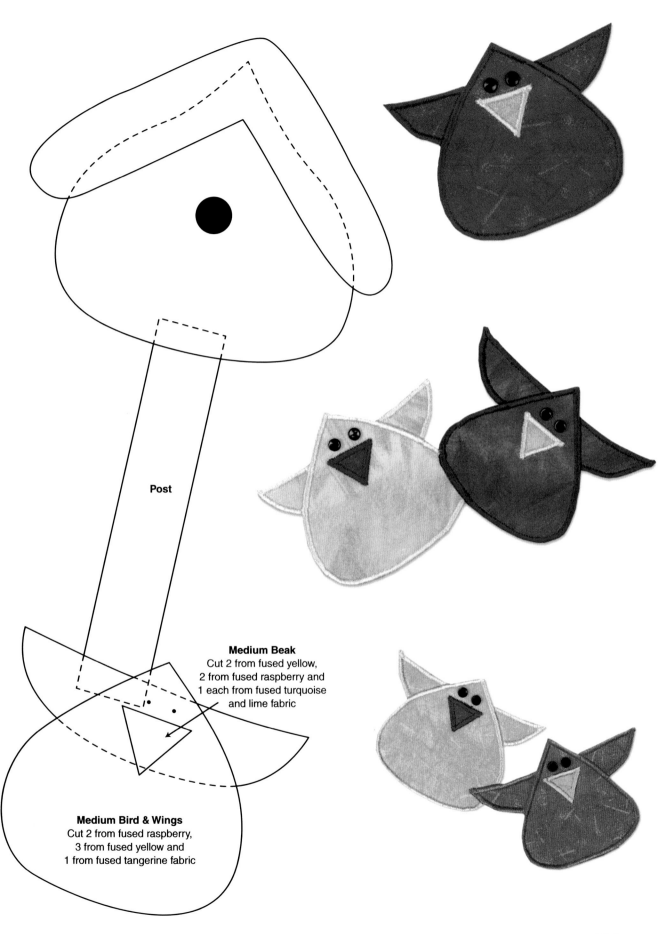

Post

Medium Beak
Cut 2 from fused yellow,
2 from fused raspberry and
1 each from fused turquoise
and lime fabric

Medium Bird & Wings
Cut 2 from fused raspberry,
3 from fused yellow and
1 from fused tangerine fabric

Simple Stamped Cap

Combine an inexpensive ball cap with economical foam stamps to create a one-of-a-kind accessory.

Design by Fran Farris

Let's Begin!

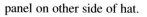

Materials

- White cotton baseball cap
- Simply Stamps set #53866 with perforated ladybug, butterfly and flower from Plaid Enterprises
- Americana fabric painting medium #DAS10 from DecoArt
- Americana acrylic paints from DecoArt: peaches 'n cream #DA23, lavender #DA34, sea aqua #DA46, lamp black #DA67, royal fuchsia #DA151 and Santa red #DA170
- Paintbrushes: #6 and #12 shaders and 5/0 spotter
- Black ultra-fine-point permanent marker
- Short glass cup with flat bottom
- White cotton baseball cap

Project Notes

Refer to photo throughout. Place each section of hat being stamped on top of an upside-down glass cup; pull fabric around cup to make a taut surface for stamping.

Instructions

1. Mix two parts paint with one part fabric painting medium.

2. Using #6 shader, apply paints to stamp:

Ladybug: Apply Santa red to body and lamp black to head; stamp on a front panel and opposite panel on back of hat.

Flower: Apply lavender to flower petals; stamp on a front panel and opposite panel on back of hat.

Butterfly: Apply peaches 'n cream; stamp on a side panel and on opposite panel on other side of hat.

3. *Backgrounds:* Using #12 shader, brush peaches 'n cream around each stamped ladybug, leaving a narrow white space around each. In same manner, paint sea aqua around each flower and royal fuchsia around each butterfly.

4. Using pointed end of #6 brush dipped in royal fuchsia, press random dots onto peaches 'n cream backgrounds; press a single dot in center of each flower. Using same method and spotter brush, paint four lamp black dots on each ladybug's body; paint black line down center of bug.

5. On each butterfly body, with lavender, paint arcs in larger parts of wings and swirls beneath; paint center line. Add a shorter sea aqua line on either side of lavender line and sea aqua arcs inside lavender arcs;

add tiny accent dots of Santa red.

6. Paint button on top of hat Santa red; let dry. Using spotter brush, paint button to look like a ladybug by adding a head at one end, a center line to define wings and tiny spots.

7. *Brim:* Paint inner section lavender. Using #12 shader, paint edge of brim in a pattern of alternating peaches 'n cream, Santa red and sea aqua stripes.

8. Using marking pen throughout, outline all stamped designs. Draw curly antennae on each ladybug; draw stem and swirling leaf under each flower, and center curl on dot in flower; draw long, curly antennae on top of each butterfly and short curls under each. Draw wavy lines between cap sections and just inside alternating pattern on brim.❀

Terrific Tennies

Save these colorful tennies for a special occasion, or just use them for decoration! Seek out leather tennies on clearance shelves. A little paint turns them into works of art!

Design by Fran Farris

Let's Begin!

Materials
- Leather or vinyl tennis shoes
- Americana acrylic paints from DecoArt: peaches 'n cream #DA23, baby pink #DA31, lavender #DA34, mint julep green #DA45, Indian turquoise #DA87 and Santa red #DA170
- Acrylic sealer/finisher spray
- Paintbrushes: #6 and #8 shaders and 5/0 spotter
- Pigma brush markers from Sakura: green and black brush pens
- Black Pigma Micron 05 pen from Sakura
- 22 pony beads in assorted colors

Project Notes
Refer to photo throughout.

Allow paints to dry between applications.

Instructions
1. Remove shoelaces from shoes before painting.

2. Using #8 shader, base-coat shoes in color blocks: paint top fronts baby pink; paint inner sides mint julep green; paint outer sides peaches 'n cream; paint back panels and front tabs (at base of lacing holes) Santa red; paint top of bottom rims Indian turquoise; paint lower bottom rims lavender.

3. Using #6 shader and lavender, paint flowers on top front: Paint five-petal shapes of various sizes (about ¾" diameter), randomly spaced. Using spotter and peaches 'n cream, paint swirl in center of each flower. Highlight edges of two or three petals with black brush pen.

4. Using mint julep green and spotter brush, paint one or two leaves next to each flower; highlight and stroke on center vein with green brush pen.

5. Using pointed end of spotter dipped in peaches 'n cream, press random dots onto mint julep green portions of shoes.

6. Using spotter and Santa red, paint small hearts randomly over peaches 'n cream sections. When dry, outline each with black marker pen.

7. Using black brush pen, draw five swirls on each back panel and one swirl on each front tab.

8. Spray all painted surfaces of shoes with acrylic sealer/finisher. Let dry.

9. String five assorted pony beads on center of each shoelace before lacing shoes; string three beads onto each shoelace end after lacing. ❦

Bizzy Bug Visors

Enjoy fun in the sun with your little one wearing these coordinating sun visors decorated in a snap with colorful craft foam.

Designs by Helen Rafson

Let's Begin!

Materials
Both Visors

- ☐ Craft foam: red, yellow and black
- ☐ Plastic sun visors: red for child's visor and yellow for adult's
- ☐ Black #31 rickrack from Wright's: baby size for child's visor and medium size for adult's
- ☐ ¼" round hole punch
- ☐ Black pompoms: 2 (½") for child's visor and 2 (¾") for adult's
- ☐ Movable eyes: 2 (10mm) for child's visor and 2 (12mm) for adult's
- ☐ Black chenille stem
- ☐ White milky gel pen
- ☐ Pinking shears or pinking-edge paper edgers
- ☐ Craft glue and craft-foam glue

Project Note
Refer to photo and patterns throughout.

Instructions
1. Cut pattern for desired visor from black craft foam; go over curved edge again with pinking shears or paper edgers.

2. Using milky gel pen, draw mouth and dashed outline on craft-foam head.

3. Using hole punch, punch one dot from red craft foam and 12 dots from black craft foam for child's visor; punch one yellow dot for adult's visor. Glue red (or yellow) dot onto black craft-foam face for nose and glue on movable eyes.

4. *Child's visor:* Cut two (2¾") pieces of baby rickrack. Glue black foam head to center front of visor, trimming bottom edge as needed and gluing rickrack in place for antennae. Glue ½" pompoms to ends of rickrack; glue black craft-foam dots randomly over surface of visor.

Adult's visor: Glue two bands of medium rickrack around visor. Cut two (3¾") pieces from chenille stem; bend into antenna shapes. Glue craft-foam head to center front of visor, trimming bottom edge as needed and gluing chenille antennae in place with ends under head. Glue ¾" pompoms to ends of chenille antennae. ❀

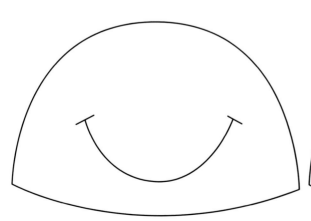

Child's Visor
Cut 1 from black
craft foam

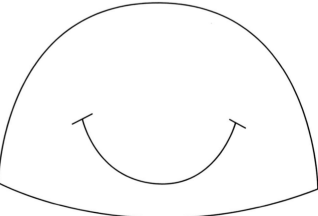

Adult's Visor
Cut 1 from black
craft foam

Blooming Clogs

Transform bargain-basement clogs into one-of-a-kind footwear with stamps and paints.

Design by Laura Scott

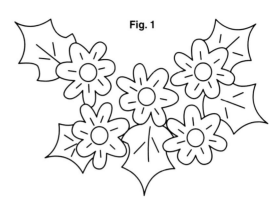

Fig. 1

Let's Begin!

Materials

- ☐ Denim clogs
- ☐ Simply Stamps from Plaid Enterprises: daisy and ivy (part of Nature Series #53897)
- ☐ Dimensional Fashion fabric paint from Plaid Enterprises: bright green shiny #25310 and red sparkle #25355
- ☐ Brush-On Fashion fabric paint from Plaid Enterprises: green apple #37423 and berry red #37408
- ☐ Fabric-painting brushes
- ☐ Scotch Gard or other sealer (optional)

Project Notes

Refer to photo and Fig. 1 throughout.

Allow paints to dry between layers and applications.

Instructions

1. Using flower stamp, stamp five berry red flowers on top front of each clog, overlapping them slightly. Using ivy leaf stamp, stamp four green apple leaves around each cluster of flowers.

2. Outline centermost flower petals and flower centers with red sparkle paint; outline remaining flowers. Outline leaves and add veins with bright green shiny paint.

3. When paints are completely dry, spray with sealer, following manufacturer's instructions. ❧

Child's Art Apron

Little ones will want to delve into the arts just for the chance to wear this fun, colorful apron!

Design by Barbara Woolley

Let's Begin!

Materials

- Child's natural canvas apron with four pockets #01153 from BagWorks
- Shimmering Fabric Colors from Delta: silver #10-401, kelly #10-404, brown #10-405, sun bright yellow #10-408, robin blue #10-409, violet #10-411, pastel blue #10-415, and holly day red #10-431
- Brush-On Fabric Colors from Delta: orange #10-303, light brown #10-315 and white #10-319
- Fabric-painting brushes: #2 and #4 flat round scrubbers, #6 flat scrubber and size 3
- Black Shiny Liner dimensional fabric paint from Delta
- Shirt painting board
- Tracing paper and/or transfer paper
- Iron

Project Note

Refer to photo and patterns throughout.

Refer to directions for "Transferring Designs" in General Instructions on page 190.

Follow manufacturer's instructions for heat-setting paints with iron.

Instructions

1. Wash and dry apron without using fabric softener; press as needed to remove wrinkles.

2. Secure apron on painting board. Transfer "WET PAINT" and two large brushes onto top portion of apron; add four freehand "blotches" of paint. Beginning on left-hand pocket and working toward right, transfer one wide brush onto left-hand pocket; add a few freehand paint drops. Transfer crisscrossing small and large paintbrushes on next pocket, paint jar and paint tube on next pocket, and one wide brush on right-hand pocket; add a few paint drops.

3. Paint "WET PAINT" design: *holly day red*—W and most of E, painted portion of bristles on top brush, one paint blotch and a few freehand paint droplets; *robin blue*—larger portion of P, painted part of bristles on bottom brush, one paint blotch and a few droplets; *white*—remaining portions of all letters; *kelly*—paint blotch and a few droplets; *sunbright yellow*—paint blotch and a few droplets; *silver*—ferules on brushes; *orange*—one paintbrush handle; *violet*—remaining handle; *brown*—brush tips.

4. Working left to right, paint pockets: *light brown*—handles on wide brushes; *brown*—unpainted bristles on all brushes; *orange*—paint on left-hand brush and a few droplets; *sunbright yellow*—paint on right-hand brush and a few droplets; *robin blue*—large brush handle; *kelly*—small brush handle; *pastel blue*—label and stripe on paint tube; *silver*—ferules on all four brushes and tube; *white*—cap and label on paint jar and cap on tube; *holly day red*—paint jar.

5. When paints have dried, add freehand swirls of holly day red and pastel blue to apron bib; add orange swirl to left-hand pocket, light green and pastel blue swirls to next pocket, pastel blue and holly day red swirls to next pocket and sunbright yellow swirls to right-hand pocket. Write "RED" on paint jar label with holly day red, and "Blue" on paint tube label with robin blue.

6. Outline designs and add details with shiny black dimensional paint.

7. Heat-set paints by ironing apron from wrong side. ❀

Paint Jar

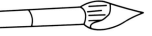

Small Brush

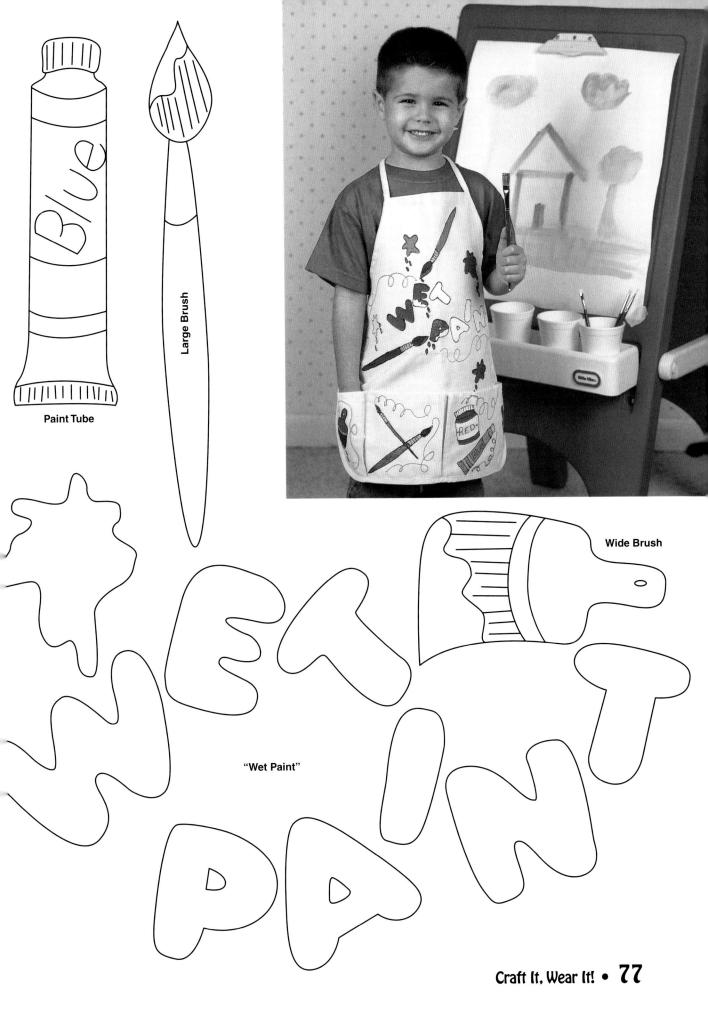

Paint Tube

Large Brush

Wide Brush

"Wet Paint"

Blue

Cat Vest

With the help of your sewing machine, adorn a denim vest with simple kitty-cat appliqués to delight the young cat lover in your family.

Design by Angie Wilhite

Materials

- ☐ Child's denim vest
- ☐ Fabric scraps: gold print and blue-and-gold plaid
- ☐ 4 (⅛") black round flat buttons
- ☐ All-purpose sewing threads: black and gold to match print fabric
- ☐ Gold rayon embroidery thread to match print fabric
- ☐ Pellon products from Plaid: ⅙ yard Wonder-Under fusible transfer web, ⅙ yard Heavy Duty Wonder-Under fusible transfer web, ⅙ yard Fusible Fleece, ⅙ yard fusible interfacing and ⅙ yard Stitch-n-Tear fabric stabilizer
- ☐ Sewing machine with satin stitch attachment
- ☐ Iron

Project Notes

Refer to photo and patterns throughout.

Follow manufacturer's instructions for using fusible products.

Instructions

1. Wash and dry vest and fabrics without using fabric softener; press as needed to remove wrinkles.

2. Fuse interfacing to back of light appliqué fabrics; fuse heavy-duty transfer web to back of gold-and-blue plaid. Apply fusible fleece to back of cat fabric, then transfer web to fleece side of same fabric.

3. Trace two cats and two tails, reversing one of each, onto paper side of fused gold print; trace seven hearts onto paper side of plaid fabric. Cut out pieces.

4. Remove paper backing; arrange cats, tails and hearts on vest fronts. Fuse in place with iron.

5. Pin or baste stabilizer inside vest fronts to cover design area. Thread sewing machine with rayon thread in top and all-purpose thread in bobbin. Satin-stitch around tails of cats, then around cat bodies. Remove fabric stabilizer; trim threads.

6. Sew two buttons to each cat's face for eyes. ❁

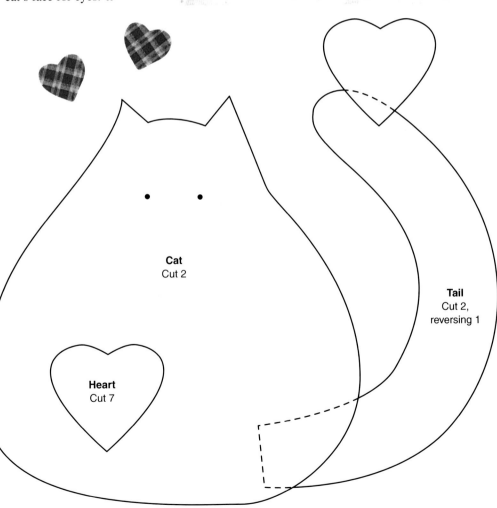

Cat
Cut 2

Tail
Cut 2,
reversing 1

Heart
Cut 7

Baby Tees

T-shirts and onesies are indispensable in the nursery! Give them a special touch with delicate applications of lace and ribbons to dress up the little lady from day one.

Designs by Chris Malone

Materials

- ☐ Pink knit baby T-shirt or onesie
- ☐ ½"- to ¾"-wide gathered white lace to fit across front of neck
- ☐ Pink embroidery floss to match shirt
- ☐ 8" piece (⅜"-wide) pink-and-white checked ribbon *or* 5" piece (¼"-wide) green satin ribbon and ⅜" white ribbon rosette
- ☐ White sewing thread
- ☐ Hand-sewing and embroidery needles
- ☐ Seam sealant (optional)

Project Note

Refer to photo throughout.

Instructions

1. Using 2 strands embroidery floss, blanket stitch over finished edge of lace to secure lace around neck front about ⅜" from neck edge.

2. *Bow trim:* Tie checked ribbon in a bow; notch ends of ribbon and apply seam sealant, if desired; let dry. Tack to center front of neckline with hand-sewing needle and thread.

Rose trim: Fold green ribbon in a figure-eight loop with ends hanging down; tack in center with hand-sewing needle and thread to secure loop. Trim ribbon ends at an angle and apply seam sealant if desired; let dry. Sew rose to center of bow and sew bow to center front of neck. ✿

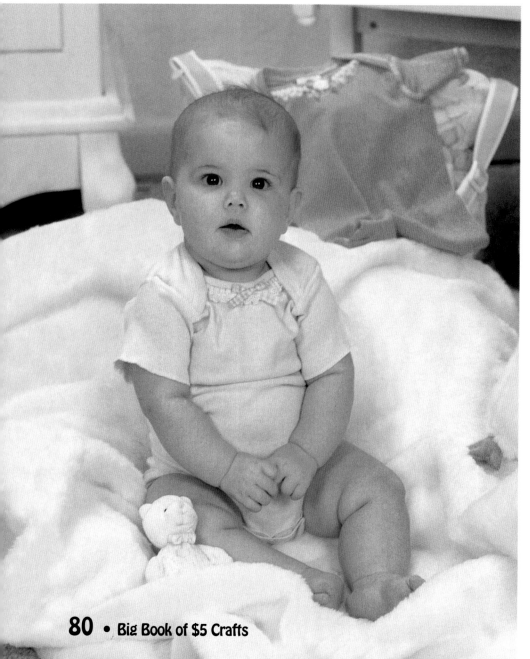

Playtime Apron

Stencil bright butterflies on a canvas apron to make a charming cover-up for playtime and arts-and-crafts projects.

Design by Mary Ayres

Project Notes
Refer to photo throughout.

Refer to instructions for stenciling under "Painting Techniques" in General Instructions on page 191.

Instructions
1. Cover binding on top of apron and 2" down each of top sides with masking tape. Place wavy edge of stencil horizontally across apron (bottom points of waves should be ¾" below binding) and tape to hold. Stencil area above wave edge with baby blue; shade bottom edge of waves with sapphire. Repeat for top of apron pocket. Remove tape.

2. Tape large butterfly with rounded wings at an angle on center top of apron. Stencil wings with spice pink, body with sable brown and antennae with sapphire. Shade edges of body and wings with sapphire. Stencil curly shapes around butterfly with olive green and dots with summer lilac.

3. Tape large butterfly with rounded wings at an angle on center of apron pocket and stencil as in step 2.

4. Tape small butterfly with rounded wings angled inward on left side of apron. Stencil wings with yellow light, body with sable brown, and antennae with sapphire. Shade body and wings with sapphire. Stencil dots in center of top wings with sapphire.

5. Tape small butterfly with pointed bottom wings angled inward on right side of apron. Stencil wings with tangerine, body with sable brown, and antennae with sapphire. Shade edges of body and wings with sapphire. Stencil dots in center of top wings with sapphire.

6. Stencil olive green curly shapes and summer lilac dots on apron pocket around small butterflies.

7. Sew buttons on large butterflies with sapphire blue floss as shown in photo. ✿

Materials
- ☐ Child's off-white canvas apron with pockets
- ☐ Plaid Simply Stencils butterfly stencil #28979
- ☐ 4 (⅝⁶") flat yellow buttons
- ☐ Americana acrylic paints from DecoArt: tangerine #DA12, spice pink #DA30, baby blue #DA42, olive green #DA56, sable brown #DA61, sapphire #DA99, yellow light #DA144 and summer lilac #DA189
- ☐ 8 (¼") stencil brushes
- ☐ Masking tape
- ☐ Sapphire blue embroidery floss
- ☐ Embroidery needle

Rickrack Bib

The plainest bib becomes a fashion statement with the addition of colorful rickrack in big, bold colors and a few simple, fun embroidery stitches.

Design by Nancy Marshall

Let's Begin!

Materials
- HeadStarts white bib with white bias trim
- Rickrack: turquoise, lime green and shocking pink
- DMC 6-strand embroidery floss: shocking pink #603, lime green #703, yellow #725, purple #3837 and turquoise #3846
- Embroidery needle

Project Notes
Refer to photo and stitch diagrams throughout.

Use 3 strands embroidery floss for all stitching unless otherwise indicated.

Instructions
1. Fold one end of turquoise rickrack under about ¼" (one point) and, using 1 strand of matching floss, sew edges together to secure.

2. Pin turquoise rickrack to bib so outer points just touch bias edging. Using shocking pink floss, make a small stitch at each rickrack point to tack it in place. Finish end of rickrack as in step 1.

3. Using same method and purple floss, tack lime rickrack around bib ½" from first piece. Tack pink rickrack in place ½" from lime piece using turquoise floss.

4. Using yellow floss, work herringbone stitch along center of lime rickrack.

5. Between points facing lime rickrack on both turquoise and pink rickrack pieces, work one purple lazy daisy with a lime straight stitch on each side. ❀

Lazy-Daisy/Straight Stitch

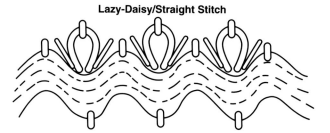

Herringbone Stitch

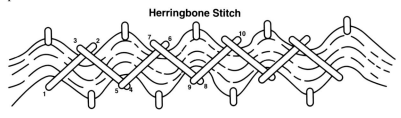

Lazy Daisy

Fish Fun Bib

It's no fish story! You *can* create this colorful bib without sewing a stitch!

Design by Nancy Marshall

Let's Begin!

Materials

- HeadStarts white bib with royal blue bias trim
- Cotton fabrics: 2½" x 3¾" blue calico, 2½" x 3" yellow calico, 2" x 3" orange calico and ¾" square black
- HeatnBond Ultra Hold iron-on adhesive from Therm O Web
- Iron

Project Note

Refer to photo and patterns throughout.

Refer to manufacturer's instructions for using iron-on adhesive.

Instructions

1. Prewash fabrics and bibs; press as needed to remove wrinkles.

2. Iron adhesive onto wrong side of fabrics.

3. Cut one body from blue fabric; cut two top/bottom fins, reversing one, from yellow fabric; cut one side fin and one tail from orange fabric; cut one eye from black.

4. Remove paper backing from appliqué pieces. Arrange fabric pieces in center of bib; fuse in place. ❀

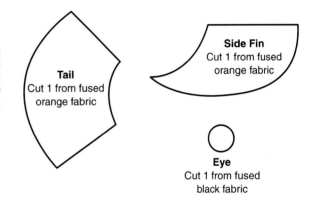

Tail
Cut 1 from fused orange fabric

Side Fin
Cut 1 from fused orange fabric

Eye
Cut 1 from fused black fabric

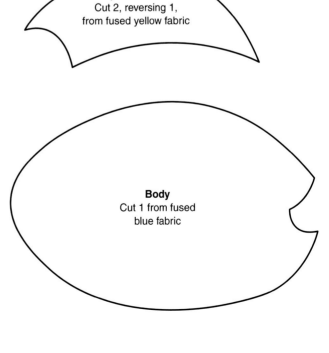

Top/Bottom Fin
Cut 2, reversing 1, from fused yellow fabric

Body
Cut 1 from fused blue fabric

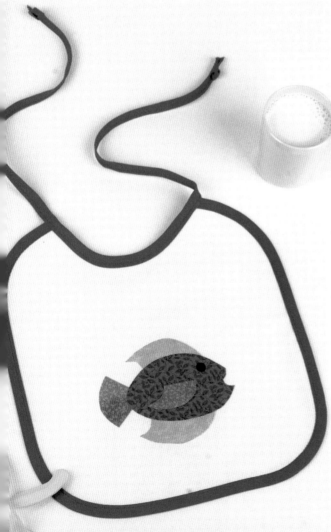

"Chicks Rule" T-Shirt

Little girls will adore this colorful T-shirt decorated with fused-on chick and egg appliqués.

Design by Sandra Graham Smith

Let's Begin!

Materials

- ☐ Girl's T-shirt
- ☐ Cotton fabric scraps in assorted solids and/or prints: yellow, navy blue, brown, white and red
- ☐ Tulip shiny black dimensional fabric paint from Duncan Enterprises
- ☐ ¼ yard HeatnBond Ultra Hold iron-on adhesive from Therm O Web
- ☐ Waxed paper
- ☐ Iron

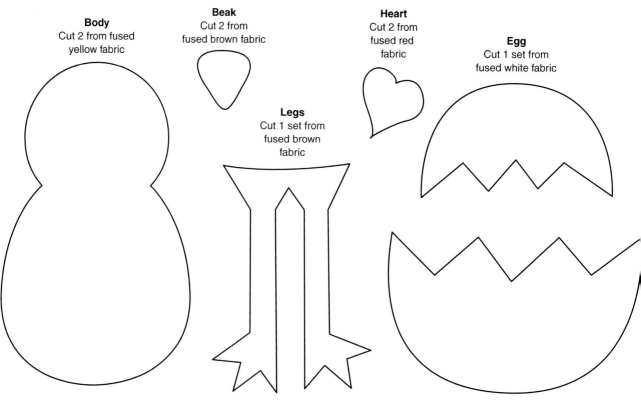

Body
Cut 2 from fused yellow fabric

Beak
Cut 2 from fused brown fabric

Heart
Cut 2 from fused red fabric

Egg
Cut 1 set from fused white fabric

Legs
Cut 1 set from fused brown fabric

Project Notes

Refer to photo and patterns throughout.

Refer to manufacturer's instructions for using fusible adhesive.

Instructions

1. Wash and dry shirt and fabrics without using fabric softener. Iron as needed to remove wrinkles.

2. Iron adhesive onto wrong side of fabrics.

3. Cut two bodies from yellow fabric; four wings, reversing two, from navy blue; one set of egg pieces from white; two beaks and one pair of legs from brown; and two hearts from red.

4. Remove paper backing from appliqué pieces. Arrange fabric pieces on front of shirt, overlapping pieces as necessary; fuse in place.

5. Place waxed paper inside shirt to keep paint from bleeding through. Using shiny black paint, dot eyes onto each chick and add "Chicks Rule" lettering and pattern of chicken tracks around neckline.

6. Let shirt lay flat until paint is completely dry. ❀

Wing
Cut 4, reversing 2, from fused navy blue fabric

Rosy Hair Set

Whip these up in no time to delight that special little miss! Vary the colors of headband and ribbon roses to match any outfit.

Designs by Nancy Marshall

Let's Begin!

Materials
Headband

- ☐ White fabric-covered headband
- ☐ Offray Ribbon Boutique ribbon roses with leaves: 1" light pink swirl #117, 2 (½") purple #465, 4 (½") shocking pink #175
- ☐ Hot-glue gun

Comb

- ☐ 2¾"-wide clear plastic hair comb
- ☐ Offray Ribbon Boutique ribbon roses with leaves: 1" French blue swirl #332, and 2 (½") light pink #117
- ☐ Hot-glue gun

Project Notes

Refer to photo throughout.

Headband

Glue swirl rose about 1" to one side of top/center point of headband. On each side, evenly spaced, glue one shocking pink rose, one purple, and another shocking pink.

Comb

Apply glue to top of comb. Glue blue rose at center, then a light pink rose on each side. ❀

Summer Sparkle Barrettes

Using metallic ribbon, you can whip up beautiful hair accessories to complement every summer outfit!

Designs by Celia Lange Designs

Let's Begin!

Materials
Both Barrettes

- 2 rectangular (1½" x 3") barrette bases
- 2 barrette clips
- ⅛"-wide flat metallic ribbon: 3 yards each pink and confetti
- 1 yard (¹⁄₁₆"-wide) white satin ribbon
- 6" lengths of pearls-by-the-yard: 2 pink and 1 light pink
- Purchased spray of pale blue pearls
- Assorted small silk flowers and leaves
- Hot-glue gun and glue sticks

Project Note
Refer to photo throughout.

Pink Barrette
1. Cut several 1" lengths of pink metallic ribbon; wrap and glue them over short ends of barrette base side by side. Use as many lengths as necessary to completely conceal short ends of barrette base.

2. Wrap long length of pink metallic ribbon continuously around and around barrette in opposite direction, beginning as close to the end as possible and gluing ends to back of barrette; lay ribbon smoothly and neatly, side by side, concealing ends of ribbons glued in place in step 1.

3. Cut 24" piece of white satin ribbon; tie it in a multiloop bow with two long streamers. Glue bow to center of barrette. Form loops from one strand pink pearls and one strand light pink pearls; glue ends to center of ribbon bow.

4. Glue assorted silk flowers and leaves over ribbon and pearls on barrette as desired.

5. Glue barrette base to wrong side of barrette.

Confetti Barrette
1. Repeat steps 1 and 2 for pink barrette, substituting confetti ribbon for pink.

2. With remaining 12" piece of white satin ribbon, form two loops and glue near one end of barrette. Form loops from one strand pink pearls; glue pink pearls and spray of blue pearls over ribbon ends.

3. Glue assorted silk flowers and leaves over ribbon and pearls on barrette as desired.

4. Repeat step 5 as for pink barrette. ❀

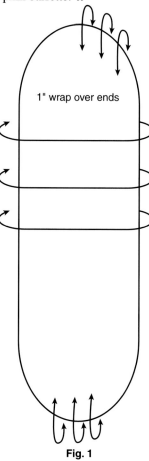

1" wrap over ends

Fig. 1

Santa Claus Brooch

This fun pin will add a delightful touch of holiday cheer to your casual outfits.

Design by Cindy Manestar

Let's Begin!

Materials

- Wooden pieces from WoodWorks: lark's loft birdhouse #CO-8425 and ½" (furniture plug) button #BR-0500
- Wavy Wool from One & Only Creations
- Ceramcoat acrylic paints from Delta: tompte red #2107, medium flesh #2126, light ivory #2401, barn red #2490 and black #2506
- Delta decorative snow paste
- Craft cement
- White tacky glue
- Hot-glue gun and glue sticks
- Stylus
- Paintbrushes: 1" wash, #1 liner and small stencil brush
- Small white glitter pompom
- 1" pin back

Project Notes

Refer to photo throughout.

Wooden birdhouse shape forms base of pin: peaked roof is hat, and body of birdhouse is Santa's face. Furniture plug button is Santa's nose.

See directions for base-coating and rouging under "Painting Techniques" in General Instructions on page 191.

Let paints and snow dry between applications.

Instructions

1. Using tacky white glue, glue furniture plug button to center of face. Using wash brush, base-coat wooden button and face with medium flesh and hat with barn red.

2. Using stencil brush, rouge cheeks with tompte red. Using stylus dipped in light ivory, add highlight dot to each cheek, and dot randomly spaced clusters of three dots onto hat. Dot on two black eyes; use liner brush to add black eyebrows. When dry, add tiny light ivory highlight dots to eyes.

3. Apply decorative snow paste along hat brim.

4. Cement pin back onto back of pin base.

5. Hot-glue strands of wool in place for beard; hot-glue pompom to tip of hat. ❊

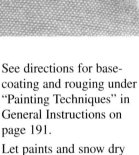

Snowman Hat

This cute chill chaser begins as a simple knit cap, and with the addition of a few simple felt shapes, is transformed into a snowman!

Design by Angie Wilhite

Let's Begin!

Materials

- Child's white knit hat with brim
- CPE felt: 4" square white #A455, 4" square black #4093, 3" square tangerine #3161, 5" square royal blue with white dots #6807
- 10" square Therm O Web HeatnBond Lite iron-on adhesive
- 6-strand cotton embroidery floss: black and white
- Embroidery needle
- Pressing paper
- Iron

Project Notes

Refer to photo and patterns throughout.

Follow manufacturer's instructions for using fusible products.

Instructions

1. Fuse adhesive to back of felt pieces.

2. Trace patterns onto paper side of fused felts: Trace two mittens, reversing one, onto blue felt; two eyes onto white; two pupils onto black and one nose onto tangerine. Cut out.

3. Position eyes and nose on hat and mittens on cuff. Cover design with pressing paper and fuse in place.

4. Using 2 strands black floss, blanket stitch around white and black portions of eyes and around nose. Using 2 strands white floss, blanket-stitch around mittens. ✿

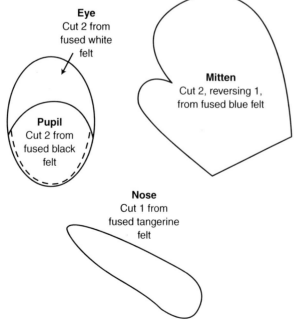

Eye
Cut 2 from fused white felt

Pupil
Cut 2 from fused black felt

Mitten
Cut 2, reversing 1, from fused blue felt

Nose
Cut 1 from fused tangerine felt

Snowman Pin

Too warm for real snowmen where you live? Keep the childlike joy of winter with this fun-and-easy, painted wooden pin.

Design by Cindy Manestar

Let's Begin!

Materials
- Wooden pieces from WoodWorks: lark's loft birdhouse #CO-8425 and ⅜" wooden furniture plug #BR-0375
- Ceramcoat acrylic paints from Delta: tompte red #2107, light ivory #2401, barn red #2490 and black #2506
- Delta decorative snow paste
- Delta sparkle glaze
- Craft cement
- Hot-glue gun and glue sticks
- Stylus
- Paintbrushes: 1" wash, #1 shader and small stencil brush
- 2 small red glitter pompoms
- 2½" piece craft wire
- Scrap of homespun fabric
- 1" pin back

Project Notes
Refer to photo throughout.

Wooden birdhouse shape forms base of pin: peaked roof is snowman's hat, and body of birdhouse is his face.

See directions for base-coating and rouging under "Painting Techniques" in General Instructions on page 191.

Let paints, glaze and snow dry between applications.

Instructions
1. Using shader, base-coat wooden plug with barn red. Using wash brush, base-coat face with light ivory and hat with black.

2. Using craft cement, glue painted wooden plug to face for nose.

3. Using stencil brush, rouge cheeks with tompte red. Using stylus dipped in light ivory, dot randomly spaced clusters of three dots onto hat. Dot on two black eyes and add mouth with smaller dots of black. When dry, add tiny light ivory highlight dots to eyes.

4. Highlight tip of nose with sparkle glaze. Apply decorative snow paste along hat brim.

5. *Earmuffs:* Bend wire over hat; hot-glue pompom to side of hat over each end of wire to hold wire in place.

6. Cement pin back onto back of pin. Tie strip of homespun fabric around neck for scarf. ❧

Friendly Frosty Apron

The white doily trim on this fun painted design mimics a snowflake.

Design by Mary Ayres

Let's Begin!

Materials

- Denim apron
- 8" round white crocheted doily from Wimpole Street Creations
- Ribbon: ½ yard (⅛") red satin and ½ yard (⅝") red-and-white polka-dot
- 2 silk holly leaves
- ⅜" white flat button
- Americana acrylic paints from DecoArt: white wash #DA2, country red #DA18, Williamsburg blue #DA40, mistletoe #DA53, lamp black #DA67, olde gold #DA176 and gingerbread #DA218
- Soft round #6 paintbrush
- ZIG Memory System black twin-tip writer from EK Success Ltd.
- Sewing threads: red, black and white
- Hand-sewing needle
- Iron
- Press cloth

Project Notes

Refer to photo and pattern throughout.

See instructions for rouging and dots under "Painting Techniques" in General Instructions on page 191.

Instructions

1. Transfer snowman pattern to center of doily. Paint as follows: *white wash*—snowman; *gingerbread*—nose; *country red*—hatband; *lamp black*—hat; *Williamsburg blue*—sky; *olde gold*—bow tie. Dot tie evenly with mistletoe.

2. When paints are dry, rouge cheeks with country red. Using side of marker's bullet tip, draw eyes and buttons; add tiny white wash highlight dots to eyes, cheeks, sky and buttons.

Add remaining details with fine tip of black marker. Heat-set paint with iron and press cloth.

3. Weave red satin ribbon through openings in crocheting around doily center beginning and ending at center bottom. Sew ribbon ends to doily to secure. Using black thread, sew button to right side of hatband at x.

4. Pin doily to center front near top of apron with top of doily 1" below top of apron. Sew doily to apron around outer edge using needle and white thread.

5. Sew bottom tips of holly leaves together at center bottom of doily, covering ribbon ends. Tie polka-dot ribbon in a bow; trim ends even and notch. Sew bow on top of holly leaves with red thread. ❀

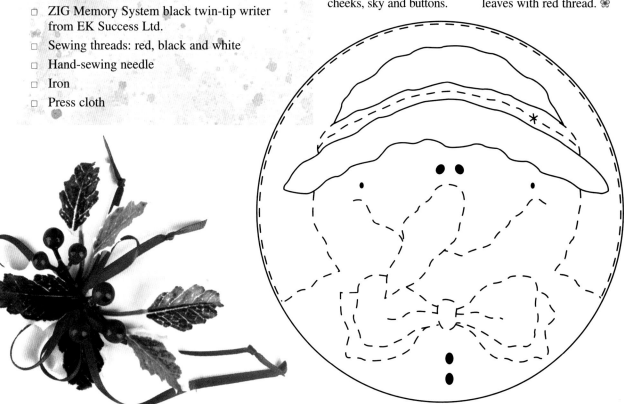

Country Snowman Vest

Fuzzy felt in heather tones and a selection of buttons combine to make a primitive-style design of snowman and stars for a beautifully simple vest.

Design by Mary Ayres

Let's Begin!

Materials

- ☐ Materials for vest (see Project Notes): commercial vest pattern with straight front, and approximately 1 yard each of lightweight wool and black cotton lining
- ☐ Squares of felt in heather tones: 1 each gold, gray and blue
- ☐ Buttons: 1 each ⅜", ½" and ¾" flat gold buttons; ½" flat gray button; and 12 assorted ½" flat off-white buttons
- ☐ Cotton embroidery floss: black and yellow-gold
- ☐ Black sewing thread
- ☐ Embroidery and sewing needles
- ☐ Iron
- ☐ Press cloth

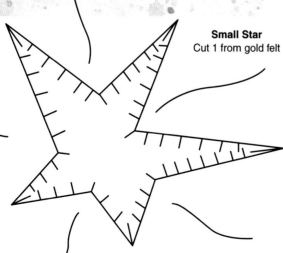

Small Star
Cut 1 from gold felt

Country Snowman Vest
Cut 1 snowman from gray felt and 1 hat from blue felt

Project Notes

Refer to photo and patterns throughout.

McCalls pattern #7173, view D, was used for sample project. Amounts of lightweight wool and lining may vary with size and style of vest.

Use 3 strands embroidery floss throughout.

Instructions

1. Wash and dry cotton and wool fabrics and felt squares without using fabric softener. Iron as needed to remove wrinkles.

2. Cut vest fronts from wool fabric; cut one each of small, medium and large stars from gold felt, one snowman from gray and hat from blue.

3. Pin large star to left front of vest 2" from center and 8" up from bottom. Pin medium star and snowman pieces to right front of vest with snowman 2" up from bottom and 1⅜" in from center at widest part. Pin small star 1½" above snowman and 1¼" in from armhole.

4. Using black floss throughout, blanket stitch around snowman stars and hat. Embroider stem stitch along arms and hat brim; embroider eyes with lazy daisy stitch.

5. Using gold floss, embroider outline stitch along star rays.

6. Using black floss throughout, sew gray button to chest dot on snowman; sew gold buttons to centers of stars, matching smallest button to smallest star, etc.; and sew off-white buttons under snowman for snow.

7. Finish vest as pattern instructs, making sure to keep a press cloth between felt and iron when ironing or felt will melt. ✿

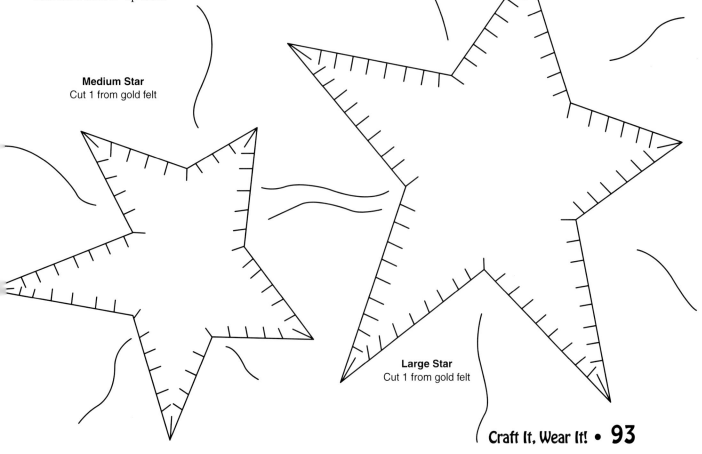

Medium Star
Cut 1 from gold felt

Large Star
Cut 1 from gold felt

Gold Blossom Vest

Create this colorful topper from a ready-made sweatshirt and add glitz with gold glitter paint.

Design by Bev Shenefield

Let's Begin!

Materials

- ☐ Magenta sweatshirt with set-in sleeves
- ☐ Magenta sewing thread
- ☐ 18 gold-tone buttons
- ☐ Jewel glue
- ☐ Tulip Designer Dye from Duncan: purple, royal purple, burgundy, lime green and teal
- ☐ Tulip gold glitter dimensional paint from Duncan
- ☐ Paintbrushes: flat and round
- ☐ Water-soluble fabric-marking pen
- ☐ Sewing machine

Project Note

Refer to photo and patterns throughout. Reverse direction of veins on some leaves.

Instructions

1. Wash and dry sweatshirt without using fabric softener. Carefully remove sleeves, knit neckband and waistband. Cut open down center front from neck to hem, rounding edges of neck and bottom. Turn under all raw edges and machine-sew with two parallel rows of stitching.

2. Using water-soluble pen, draw pattern of flowers and leaves down both vest fronts, using patterns cut from cardboard if desired. From top to bottom, sample design includes large leaf, large flower, small leaf, medium flower, small leaf, small flower, large flower, large leaf, medium flower and small flower, small leaf, small flower and medium flower, large flower and large leaf. Vary your arrangement as desired.

3. Mix dye with enough water to allow it to spread a little but not excessively. (Use dye straight from the bottle, if you prefer.) Paint large flowers royal purple, medium flowers purple and small flowers burgundy. Paint large leaves lime green with teal blended into the centers. Paint small leaves lime green. Using round brush, dab teal and lime green around leaves and flowers. Let dyes dry thoroughly.

4. Using gold glitter dimensional paint, outline flowers and leaves; add dots in random clusters of three to background between flowers and leaves.

5. Glue buttons in centers of flowers. ❀

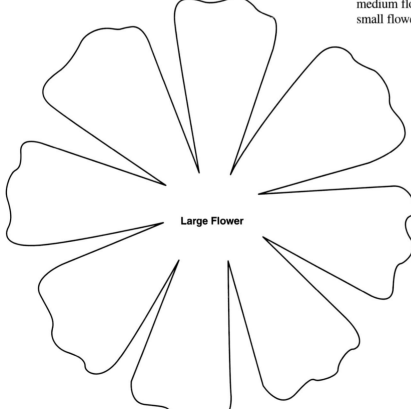

Large Flower

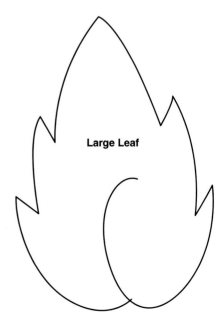

Large Leaf

Small Leaf

Small Flower

Medium Flower

Bazaar Fun

Add an extra jingle to your
pocket with this collection of
delightful bazaar crafts! The
projects in this chapter show
you how to keep your costs low
by using up odds and
ends, and recycled
cans and bottles!

Garden Guest Pincushions

Transform scraps of fabric and pompoms into a trio of colorful pincushions to keep handy by your sewing machine, ironing board and bureau.

Designs by Helen Rafson

Project Note

Refer to photo throughout.

General Assembly

1. Cut plastic foam ball in half with serrated knife; reserve one half for another use.

2. Cut ¼" slits evenly around 6½" circle of fabric. Center foam half-ball on wrong side of fabric, flat side up. Cover half-ball smoothly with fabric, folding clipped edges over onto flat side and gluing them in place; let dry. Glue 2½" circle of fabric onto bottom (flat side) of body; let dry.

3. Finish pincushion as directed for individual design.

Turtle

1. Glue large pompom to edge of half-ball for head; glue on small pompoms for legs. Let dry.

2. *Tail:* Fold 2" piece of chenille stem in half; curve slightly and glue ends to underside of body. Let dry.

3. Glue eyes onto head; cut 1¼" piece embroidery floss and glue in place on head for smile.

Ladybug

1. Using cotton-tip swab dipped in black paint, dot spots onto fabric-covered body; let dry.

2. Glue black satin ribbon down center of body, gluing ends to underside. Let dry.

Let's Begin!

Materials

Each Pincushion
- 3" plastic foam ball
- Serrated knife
- Tacky craft glue
- 2 (8mm) round black wiggle eyes

Turtle
- 6½" and 2½" circles of green print fabric
- Green pompoms: 1½" and 4 (1")
- Green chenille stem
- Black embroidery floss

Ladybug
- 6½" and 2½" circles of red print fabric
- Black acrylic paint
- Cotton-tip swab
- Black pompoms: 1½" and 2 (7mm)
- 5" piece (⅛"-wide) black satin ribbon
- Black fabric-covered wire
- Red embroidery floss

Bumblebee
- 6½" and 2½" circles of yellow print fabric
- 2" miniature heart-shaped Battenburg doily from Wimpole Street Creations
- Black pompoms: 1½" and 2 (7mm)
- 12" black medium rickrack
- Black chenille stem
- Black fabric-covered wire
- Yellow embroidery floss
- Seam sealant

3. Glue large pompom to edge of half-ball for head; let dry.

4. Glue eyes onto head; cut 1¼" piece embroidery floss and glue in place for smile.

5. *Antennae:* Cut two 3" pieces of fabric-covered wire; coil around pencil. Slide coils off pencil and stretch them out a bit. Glue a 7mm pompom to

one end of each and glue other end to head. Let dry.

Bumblebee

1. Cut rickrack in half and glue each piece across fabric-covered body, gluing ends to underside. Let dry.

2. Cut 1¼" piece from chenille stem; treat ends with seam sealant and let dry. Glue one end to underside of body for stinger.

3. Cut doily in half down center. Glue to underside of body along cut edges, allowing rounded edges to protrude along sides for wings (point of heart should point toward stinger).

4. Glue large pompom to opposite edge of half-ball for head; let dry.

5. Glue eyes onto head; cut 1¼" piece embroidery floss

and glue in place for smile.

6. *Antennae:* Cut two 3" pieces of fabric-covered wire; coil around pencil. Slide coils off pencil and stretch them out a bit. Glue a 7mm pompom to one end of each and glue other end to head. Let dry. ❀

Summer Straw Hat

Bedecked with blooms and a delicate butterfly, this summery chapeau is a wonderful accent for guest bath or boudoir.

Design by Celia Lange Designs

Let's Begin!

Materials
- ☐ 6"-diameter straw hat
- ☐ 9" piece of miniature green garland with white flowers
- ☐ 8" lengths of ⅛"-wide satin ribbon: 2 rose and 1 each light pink and lavender
- ☐ Assorted small silk flowers
- ☐ 1¼" feather butterfly
- ☐ Hot-glue gun and glue sticks

Project Note
Refer to photo throughout.

Instructions
1. Wrap brim of hat with garland; glue in place.

2. Tie ribbon strands in bows; glue to center back of hat and trim ends.

3. Glue assorted small silk flowers to ribbons and around garland. Glue butterfly to crown of hat near top. ❀

Garden Pal Plant Pokes

While you're waiting for the blooms to begin, these painted plant pokes will add color and interest to your flowerbeds and borders.

Designs by Bev Shenefield

Let's Begin!

Materials

Each Plant Poke
- ☐ Wooden half-balls: 1 each 1¼"- and 2½"-diameter
- ☐ 12" piece (¼"-diameter) wooden dowel
- ☐ Sandpaper
- ☐ Tack cloth
- ☐ Craft cement
- ☐ Craft saw
- ☐ Drill with ¼" bit
- ☐ Paintbrushes: #12 flat and 20/0 script liner
- ☐ Toothpick
- ☐ Interior/exterior satin varnish

Ladybug
- ☐ #3 watercolor brush
- ☐ Ceramcoat acrylic paints from Delta: fire red #2083, white #2505 and black #2506

Turtle
- ☐ Ceramcoat acrylic paints from Delta: white #2505, black #2506, apple green #2065 and pine green #2526

Project Notes

Refer to photo and painting diagrams throughout.

Let all paints, glue and varnish dry between applications.

Instructions

1. Using saw, trim a tiny slice from edge of smaller half-ball (head) and larger half-ball (body) so they can be glued together securely.

2. Sand half-balls as needed; wipe off dust with tack cloth.

3. Paint as instructed before continuing to steps 4 and 5.

4. Drill ¼"-deep hole in center of flat side on body. Glue flattened edge of head to edge of body. Let dry completely.

5. Sharpen one end of dowel; glue other end into hole in body. Apply varnish to all painted surfaces.

Ladybug

1. Using flat brush, paint body fire red; paint head black.

2. Using #3 watercolor brush, paint black sections on body; dot on black spots with paintbrush handle dipped in black.

3. Using white paint throughout, dot eyes onto ladybug's head with paintbrush handle; using liner brush, add smile and antennae. Using toothpick, dot black pupils onto eyes.

Turtle

1. Using flat brush, paint body and head apple green.

2. Using liner brush and pine green, paint shell marks on body and add eyebrows, nose and mouth to head.

3. Using paintbrush handle, dot black eyes onto head. Using toothpick, dot white pupils onto eyes. ✿

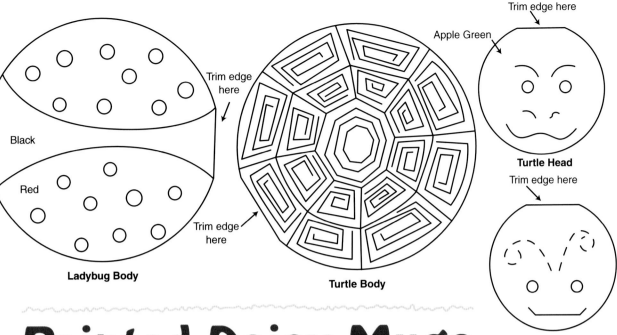

Black

Red

Ladybug Body

Trim edge here

Trim edge here

Turtle Body

Trim edge here

Apple Green

Turtle Head

Trim edge here

Ladybug Head

Painted Daisy Mugs

Ceramic mugs are inexpensive and fun to decorate with easy-to-use enamel paints.

Design by Beth Wheeler

Project Notes

Refer to photo throughout.

Do not mix or thin paints with water.

Remove smudges with stylus, toothpick or cotton-tip swab.

Wash flat paintbrush and pouncer brush with warm water before paint dries.

Allow paint to dry for 24 hours before heat-setting paints in a home oven.

Instructions

1. Wash mugs thoroughly
Continued on page 111

Let's Begin!

Materials

- ☐ Plain white ceramic mug
- ☐ Ultra Gloss air-dry enamel paints from DecoArt: cadmium yellow #DG06, Christmas red #DG10, Christmas green #DG11 and true blue #DG30
- ☐ Easy Cling pouncer brush from DecoArt or cotton-tip swab
- ☐ Flat paintbrush
- ☐ White vinegar

Green Thumb Gardening Angel

Everyone knows someone who dotes on a garden, so everyone knows someone who would love this whimsical gal. Magical sprinkles flow from her watering can, and her "wand" is topped with a tiny birdhouse!

Design by Angie Wilhite

Pattern Notes

Allow paints and finishes to dry thoroughly between coats.

Refer to photo and pattern throughout.

Instructions

1. Launder fabrics without using fabric softener.

2. Sand dowel; wipe with tack cloth. Spray dowel and head bead with gloss sealer. Paint head dusty rose and dowel terra cotta. Spray both pieces with gloss sealer again. Glue head to top of breath mints container.

3. Holding gold fabric pieces together right sides facing, sew along both long sides and one short end using ¼" seam allowance. Clip corners; turn right side out and press. Trim open edge of bag with pinking shears.

4. With coordinating thread, sew gathering stitch around mouth of bag ⅜" from pinked edge, leaving thread tails. Insert breath mints container into bag; add polyester fiberfill to fill bag and hold container in center. Pull ends of gathering thread snugly around doll's neck; knot.

5. Remove shanks from buttons. Glue birdhouse to one end of dowel; glue watering can to bottom right corner of angel's dress.

6. Cut jute hair in half; glue in place atop bead head. Glue on hat and glue eyes to face; draw smile with fine-line marking pen.

7. Following manufacturer's instructions, fuse fleece to back of one green fabric piece and transfer web to back of the other. Remove paper backing; sandwich pieces together, web facing fleece, and fuse. Cut one pair of wings from fused fabric; glue to back of dress.

8. Fold cream ribbon in half; tie square knot in center and glue ends to back of neck so ribbon "arms" extend around front. Position dowel with birdhouse in arms; glue dowel to dress.

9. Tie green ribbon in a bow; trim ends and glue over gathering stitches at neck. ❁

Let's Begin!

Materials
Each Angel

- □ 4" piece (⅛"-diameter) wooden dowel
- □ 1¼"-diameter wooden head bead from Forster
- □ Americana acrylic paints from DecoArt: dusty rose #DA25 and terra cotta #DA62
- □ Americana gloss acrylic sealer/finisher #DAS12 from DecoArt
- □ Empty plastic Tic-Tac breath mints container
- □ 3" straw hat
- □ Fabric: 2 (4" x 3") pieces gold print, and 2 (4" x 8") pieces green print
- □ Polyester fiberfill
- □ Sewing thread to match gold fabric
- □ Hand-sewing needle
- □ Decorative buttons: watering can and birdhouse
- □ 11" jute curly hair
- □ 2 (7mm) round black wiggle eyes
- □ Fine-tip black permanent marking pen
- □ 4" x 8" piece Pellon Fusible Fleece
- □ 4" x 8" piece Pellon Heavy-Duty Wonder-Under transfer web
- □ ⅛"-wide satin ribbon: 6" green and 7" cream
- □ Paintbrush
- □ Craft cement
- □ Fine sandpaper
- □ Tack cloth
- □ Pinking shears or rotary cutter with pinking blade
- □ Iron

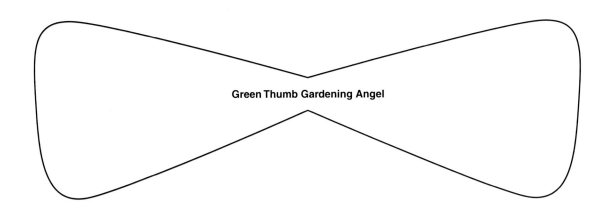

Green Thumb Gardening Angel

Victorian Lavender Sachet

Sweeten closets and dresser drawers with the lovely aroma of lavender encased in a pretty sachet you've dressed up with ribbons and flowers.

Design by Celia Lange Designs

Project Note
Refer to photo throughout.

Instructions
1. Fill sachet with lavender and stitch closed.

2. Glue two or three silk leaves at base of hanging loop. Tie ribbon strands in bows; glue to leaves and trim ends.

3. Glue assorted small silk flowers to ribbons. ❀

Let's Begin!

Materials
- 4"-diameter white lace sachet
- Dried lavender
- 18" lengths of ¼"-wide picot-edge satin ribbon: 1 each light pink, rose and yellow
- Assorted small silk leaves and flowers to match ribbon
- Hand-sewing needle and white thread
- Hot-glue gun and glue sticks

Potted Pincushion

These whimsical helpers for the sewing table and bureau are easy to make from scraps of fabric and felt, and tiny terra-cotta flowerpots.

Design by Barbara Woolley

Pattern Notes

Refer to photo throughout.

Refer to manufacturer's instructions for using fusible web.

Let sealer and paints dry before proceeding to next step.

Instructions

1. Spray flowerpot with acrylic sealer. Paint craft stick green; paint rim of flowerpot using color to coordinate with flower fabric; paint "PINS" on front of flowerpot, adding dots to ends of letters with tip of paintbrush handle dipped in paint.

2. Pin flower fabric to coordinating felt, wrong sides facing. Cut through both layers to make a simple 4" flower shape. By hand or machine, stitch flower halves together, using ⅛" seam allowance and leaving opening at bottom for stuffing.

3. Stuff flower with fiberfill, pushing it into petals with a long, blunt object like the eraser end of a pencil. Hand-stitch opening closed.

4. Position buttons in center of flower, one on each side. Using coordinating embroidery floss, stitch through button, flower and other button several times to attach buttons and indent center of flower. Bury thread end inside flower.

5. With sharp pointed scissors, carefully cut a ⅜" horizontal slit near bottom edge of flower on felt side; apply a little glue to one end of painted craft stick and insert into flower.

6. Fuse green felt to leaf fabric, wrong sides facing. Using pinking shears, cut two simple leaves, 1" x 2", from fused layers. Glue base of leaves to craft stick stem so that fabric side faces front on one side and felt side faces front on the other.

7. Trim plastic foam to fill flowerpot; glue in place. Apply a little glue to end of craft stick and stick into foam so that fabric side of flower faces front. Cover top of foam with glued-on scraps of sheet moss. Tie torn fabric strip in a bow around base of craft stick stem; glue in place on back of bow. ❧

Let's Begin!

Materials
Each Pincushion

- ☐ 2½"-diameter terra-cotta flowerpot
- ☐ Acrylic sealer
- ☐ Craft stick
- ☐ Fabric in country-style check or print: 5" square and matching 1" x 12" torn strip for flower; and 4" square green for leaves
- ☐ Felt: 5" square to coordinate with flower fabric; and 4" square green to coordinate with leaf fabric
- ☐ Small pieces fusible web
- ☐ Polyester fiberfill
- ☐ 2 (¾"-diameter) flat white buttons
- ☐ Hand-sewing needle and white thread
- ☐ 6-strand embroidery floss to coordinate with flower fabric
- ☐ Small piece of plastic craft foam
- ☐ Craft paints: color to coordinate with fabric, and green
- ☐ Small paintbrush
- ☐ Scraps of dried green sheet moss
- ☐ Pinking shears
- ☐ Hot-glue gun
- ☐ Sewing machine (optional)

Easy Tile Magnets

These magnets have a sophisticated, contemporary look. They're easy to create with gold stickers, tile squares and paints.

Design by Barbara Woolley

Project Notes

Refer to photo throughout.

Follow manufacturer's instructions for using surface conditioner, paints and glaze.

Instructions

1. Wash and dry tile.

2. Using larger paintbrush, brush surface conditioner over tile; let dry without wiping off excess.

3. Apply sticker to face of tile; rub with a paper towel to insure good adhesion.

4. Using smaller paintbrush, dab paints into sections of sticker without painting over raised outlines. Let dry and apply a second coat if needed.

5. Apply gloss glaze one drop at a time over each painted section. Try to give each section of the painted sticker a smooth, domed look. Let dry.

6. Glue ribbon neatly around edge of tile, trimming off excess.

7. Cement magnet to back of tile. ❀

Let's Begin!

Materials
Each Magnet

- ☐ 2"-square black ceramic tile
- ☐ 9" piece (⅛"-wide) metallic gold ribbon
- ☐ Paintbrushes: #3 round and ½" angular
- ☐ Gold Class A Peels stickers from Mark Enterprises in desired motifs
- ☐ PermEnamel Surface Conditioner and Clear Gloss Glaze from Delta
- ☐ PermEnamel Air-Dry paints from Delta in desired colors
- ☐ Window cleaner or white vinegar
- ☐ White tacky glue
- ☐ Button magnet
- ☐ Craft cement

Mini Favor Bags

Fancy paper punches and scraps of construction paper transform plain little brown paper bags into colorful party keepsakes.

Designs by Laura Scott

Let's Begin!

Materials
Each Bag
- ☐ 3¾" x 5⅝" brown paper gift bag with handles
- ☐ Black chisel-tip marker
- ☐ Glue

Happy Birthday
- ☐ Fine-tip markers: red, blue, green and black
- ☐ Construction paper: red, blue and green
- ☐ Star paper punch

Just for You
- ☐ Construction paper: pink, yellow and orange
- ☐ Fine-tip markers: green and black
- ☐ Daisy paper punch

Project Note
Refer to photo and Figs. 1–4 throughout.

Happy Birthday
1. Punch four stars each from red, blue and green construction paper. Glue stars across top and bottom of bag.

2. Using black fine-tip marker, draw face on each star (Fig. 1). Using chisel-tip marker, outline star and add accents (Fig. 2).

3. In center of bag, write "HAPPY BIRTHDAY" with chisel-tip marker. Using red, blue and green fine-tip markers, add stars to ends of letters.

Just for You
1. Using fine-tip black marker, draw wavy line along left side of bag for vine (Fig. 3). Draw small wavy lines for vines in upper right and lower right corners. Loosely trace over black line and add leaves using green marker. Outline leaves with black marker. ***Note: Do not be exact with vine leaves and outlining.***

2. Punch six daisies each from orange and yellow and five from pink. Glue daisies on vine across left side and in upper right and lower right corners.

3. Using fine-tip black marker, draw smiley face and petal accents on each daisy (Fig. 4).

4. Using chisel-tip marker, write "Just for You!" on right side of bag, adding dots to ends of letters. ✿

Fig. 1

Fig. 2 **Fig. 4**

Fig. 3

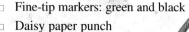

Miss Whimsy Pin

This adorable pin is a great way to use up leftovers from bigger projects. Host a pin-making "party" and ask everyone to bring their own cache of crafting goodies. You'll have a wonderful assortment of pins, and no two will be alike.

Design by Judy Atwell

Project Note

Refer to photo throughout.

Let paints and glue dry between applications.

Instructions

1. Paint edges and one side of wooden square Caribbean blue; paint one side and edges of oval with butter cream with medium paintbrush.

2. With a pencil, trace the outline of the lower portion of the oval onto one corner of the painted side of the square.

3. Cut about five pieces of dark fabric into 3¾" crescents. Glue one end of crescents to painted surface of square, placing tips inside penciled outline so the ends will be concealed when oval face is glued on later. Press this first layer smooth and flat to conceal square background.

4. Cut a second layer of six shorter crescents and glue the tips over the first layer; press down tightly.

5. From sheer fabric cut eight petal shapes; glue these on top of and between fabric crescents. Add two or three short crescents on top of the sheer petals.

6. Glue strands of ribbon on top, fanning them across fabrics.

7. Glue painted oval over corner of decorated wooden square, first padding the painted face with a scrap of cloth and then clamping the pieces together with a clothespin. Because of the many layers of fabric on the square, a space will be formed at the top between the oval and the square. Let this joining dry.

8. Using glue gun through step 9, glue two loops of beads in the space behind the oval, letting them hang down over fabrics.

9. Glue on cord with one end hanging free; then come around to the front of the oval to form a loop and continue the cord in a second row across to the right side. This cord forms the front hair. Continue making loops around the back of the oval to finish hair; trim cord. Let glue from glue gun run down into the space as you form the hair; the cord will cover this.

Let's Begin!

Materials

- Wooden cutouts: 1¼" square and 1½" egg/oval
- Ceramcoat acrylic paints from Delta: phthalo blue #2502, butter cream #2523 and Caribbean blue #2530
- 12" piece round twisted silky craft cord
- 1" silk ribbon rose
- Several scraps of shiny, glittery fabrics, including some deep colors and some sheers
- Assorted coordinating ¼" and ⅛" ribbons
- Beaded and pearl trims as desired
- Pin back
- Round paintbrushes: tiny and medium
- Spring clothespin
- Hot-glue gun and glue sticks
- Tacky craft glue
- Toothpicks

10. Tie ⅛" ribbon over cord hanging in front; tie in a bow and glue the knot. Loosen braid under the bow.

11. Glue the rose on top of the cord hair. Hold it tightly as glue cools to form the rose to the head.

12. Use the tiny brush and phthalo blue to add eyes: Paint a tiny dot with a light crescent over the tops; let dry.

13. Turn square over and glue pin back to upper corner of square. ❀

Craft Stick Frames

Those versatile craft sticks and simple wooden cutouts make wonderful frames for children's school photos. Add a strip of magnet on the back to display on the fridge, if you wish.

Designs by Fran Farris

Let's Begin!

Materials
Each Frame
- ☐ 12 wooden craft sticks
- ☐ Paintbrushes: #8 medium shader, #4 small shader and #0 round liner
- ☐ Acrylic finishing spray
- ☐ Craft glue
- ☐ Black dual-point permanent marking pen
- ☐ 1" sawtooth hanger
- ☐ Masking tape

Birds & Flowers Frame
- ☐ Precut wooden shapes: 2 (1") doves and 3 (1") flower shapes
- ☐ Americana acrylic paints from DecoArt: peaches 'n cream #DA23, baby pink #DA31, royal fuchsia #DA151, summer lilac #DA189 and primary yellow #DA201

Summer Fruits Frame
- ☐ Precut wooden shapes: 3 mini split apples and 2 (1⅜" x ⅞") melon slices
- ☐ Americana acrylic paints from DecoArt: titanium white #DA1, bright green #DA54, royal fuchsia #DA151, primary red #DA199 and primary yellow #DA201

Project Note
Refer to photo throughout.

Assemble Frame
Draw 1½" square on a piece of white paper; this will serve as a guide for the opening in the finished frame. Lay three craft sticks side by side along top edge of square; lay three more side by side along bottom edge. Lay three more side by side along left side of square on top of sticks at top and bottom, applying a little glue to the back of each stick before placing it in position. Repeat on right side of frame. Let glue dry thoroughly.

Birds & Flowers Frame
1. Using #8 shader, paint frame front and back with royal fuchsia. Position frame so top layers of sticks are at top and bottom.

2. Using #4 shader, paint fronts and sides of wooden shapes: Paint birds, reversing one, with summer lilac; paint one flower each with baby pink, primary yellow and peaches 'n cream.

3. Glue peach flower at top left of frame, yellow flower at right center and pink flower at bottom left. Glue one bird to left center and another off-center at top of frame.

4. Using fine point of black pen, draw broken outline around edges of flowers and doves. Draw swirl in center of each flower and dot eye onto each bird. Print name on frame.

Summer Fruits Frame
1. Using #8 shader, paint frame front and back with primary yellow. Position frame so top layers of sticks are on sides.

2. Using #4 shader, paint fronts and sides of wooden shapes: Paint apples primary red; paint white comma

highlights with #0 liner. Paint centers of melon halves with royal fuchsia and edges with bright green.

3. Glue one apple at top center, another at right and third in bottom left corner. Glue one melon at top left and second at bottom right.

4. Using fine point of black pen, draw seeds onto melons; print name on frame. Using #0 liner, paint bright green stem on frame above each apple.

Finishing

1. Spray frame with light coating of acrylic spray.

2. Attach sawtooth hanger to center top of frame on back.

3. Secure photo in frame opening with masking tape. ❀

Ladybug Magnets

Ladybugs are said to bring good luck. These little bugs will certainly bring good luck to your bazaar table in the form of lots of sales!

Design by Bonnie Lester

Project Notes

Refer to photo throughout.

Let glue, paints and ink dry between applications.

Follow manufacturer's instructions for using sealer.

Instructions

1. Cut ⅓ from a 2-ounce block of red modeling compound; knead until soft and pliable. Shape into a ball. Cut in half with razor; lay one piece flat side down; return other half to block of compound.

2. Indent line down center of half-ball with toothpick to define wings. Using end of dowel as a stamp, lightly press four or five indentations onto each wing; these serve as outlines for paint dots.

3. *Head:* Cut ½ from 2-ounce bar of black modeling compound; knead until soft and pliable. Shape

into a ball and press onto front of ladybug's body. Using toothpick, poke two small holes ¼" apart in top for antennae.

4. Bake ladybug on an ovenproof plate in a pre-heated 275-degree oven for 20 minutes; let cool.

5. Fill in dots on wings with black paint marker. Paint eyes on face with white paint marker; dot black pupils in centers.

6. Heat one end of plastic cord with lighter or flame so that it forms a ball; cut off piece ¼" from end. Repeat to make two antennae. Apply super glue to cut ends and insert in holes in head.

7. Spray ladybug with clear acrylic gloss coating. When dry, peel backing from magnet and press onto flat side of ladybug. ❀

Let's Begin!

Materials

- ☐ Sculpey III modeling compound: black #042 and red #083
- ☐ Speedball Painters paint markers: black #7326 and white #31332
- ☐ Small piece (1mm) black plastic "leather" cord from Crafts Etc.
- ☐ Clear acrylic gloss coating from Crafts Etc.
- ☐ ¾" Mega Strong Magnet Square with peel-and-stick foam adhesive #12331 from Magnetic Specialty Inc.
- ☐ Single-edge razor blade
- ☐ 3" piece (¼"-diameter) wooden dowel
- ☐ Toothpick
- ☐ Super glue
- ☐ Ovenproof plate
- ☐ Oven

Pressed Flower Magnets

Sandwich tiny dried flowers between plastic squares and finish with foil tape for an elegant magnet.

Design by Fran Farris

Project Note

Refer to photo throughout.

Instructions

1. Cut 2 (2") squares from plastic with craft knife. Lay one plastic square on flat surface. Using tweezers, arrange greenery and then pressed flower(s) in a tiny arrangement on plastic square. Use a toothpick to apply tiny dots of craft glue to back of greenery and flowers, using just enough glue to hold them in place.

2. Lay second plastic square over finished arrangement. Cut silvered foil strips slightly longer than 2" and apply to each edge of plastic, joining pieces of plastic with strips. Trim edges.

3. Glue magnet to back. ❀

Let's Begin!

Materials
Each Magnet

- ☐ Aleene's Crafting Plastic
- ☐ Assorted pressed flowers from Nature's Pressed
- ☐ Silvered foil from Plaid Enterprises
- ☐ Tweezers
- ☐ Craft knife
- ☐ Toothpick
- ☐ White craft glue
- ☐ Small round magnet

Pressed Flower Ornaments

These ornaments are easy to make by the dozen! Just sandwich an arrangement of pressed flowers between laminating sheets and trim the edges with silvered foil.

Design by Fran Farris

Project Note
Refer to photo throughout.

Instructions
1. Cut laminating sheet in half to make two 4" x 3" pieces.

2. Open laminating sheet on a flat surface and lay on top of 3" paper square; the paper square will serve as a guide for arranging the flowers. Lift off backing sheet to expose sticky side. Using tweezers, arrange greenery and then pressed flower(s) in a tiny arrangement on plastic.

3. Place top sheet over flower arrangement. Roll evenly across flowers while applying slight pressure. Smooth edges gently around flowers; trim to 3" square.

4. Cut silvered foil strips slightly longer than 3" and apply to each edge of ornament. Trim edges.

5. Punch hole in one corner of ornament. Thread a hanging loop of ribbon through hole. ❀

Let's Begin!

Materials
Each Ornament

☐ Half of a 4" x 6" photo laminating sheet from 3M

☐ 3" square cut from plain white paper

☐ Assorted pressed flowers from Nature's Pressed

☐ Silvered foil from Plaid Enterprises

☐ Tweezers

☐ Hole punch

☐ Ribbon scraps

Painted Daisy Mugs continued from page 101

with hot, soapy water. Rinse; dry. Clean exterior of mugs with white vinegar; allow to dry.

2. Squeeze puddles of Christmas red and cadmium yellow paints onto paper plate. Double-load flat paintbrush and stroke back and forth on paper towel to blend colors slightly.

3. Touch paintbrush tip to surface of mug; rotate to make a petal. Repeat to make five petals to complete one flower. Add additional flowers to mug as desired.

4. Dip end of pouncer in Christmas red paint; dot randomly onto surface of mug and handle.

5. Repeat steps 2–4 on remaining mugs, substituting true blue for random dots on one mug and Christmas green for dots on third.

6. Let paints dry for 24 hours. Bake mugs in a 325-degree oven as directed by paint manufacturer for dishwasher-safe finish. ❀

Garden Markers

How does your garden grow? In neat and orderly rows, with a little help from these durable, colorful markers.

Designs by Bev Shenefield

Let's Begin!

Materials
All Markers

- ☐ 14 wooden paint-stirring sticks
- ☐ Spray paint: gray primer and flat black
- ☐ Pigma Micron .03 black fine-tip pen
- ☐ Ceramcoat acrylic paints from Delta: Seminole green #2009, purple #2015, burnt umber #2025, pumpkin #2042, bright red #2503, yellow #2504, white #2505 and black #2506
- ☐ Gloss exterior varnish
- ☐ Toothpick or skewer
- ☐ Scruffy paintbrush
- ☐ Paintbrushes: size 1 spotter and size 10/0 liner
- ☐ Sandpaper
- ☐ Tack cloth
- ☐ Chalk pencil

Project Note

Refer to photo and patterns (page 114) throughout.

Instructions

1. Sand paint stirrers and wipe off dust. If lettering cannot be sanded off, use that side for back side.

2. Spray all surfaces of paint stirrers with primer; let dry thoroughly. Spray with flat black paint and let dry again.

3. Using chalk pencil, trace vegetables onto straight end (stirring end) of each stick and add lettering: "ASPARAGUS," "CORN," "BROCCOLI," "PEAS," "POTATOES," "CARROTS," "RADISHES," "TURNIPS," "LETTUCE," "CUCUMBERS," "BEETS," "ONIONS," "TOMATOES" and "PEPPERS."

4. Paint vegetables:

Asparagus—Paint Seminole green; shade with a mixture of black and Seminole green and highlight with a mixture of Seminole green and white.

Corn—Paint husks Seminole green; shade and highlight as for asparagus. Paint kernels yellow; highlight around kernels with white, then outline two sides of kernels with Pigma pen.

Broccoli—Using scruffy brush dipped in Seminole green, black and white, dab on broccoli crowns. Paint stems Seminole green; highlight as for asparagus.

Peas—Paint Seminole green; shade and highlight as for asparagus. Use liner with Seminole green tipped with mixed white and Seminole green to paint tendrils.

Potatoes—Mix burnt umber and white; paint first potato with mixture. Paint second with a mixture of bright red, white and burnt umber. Highlight by adding more white to the mixture. Dot eyes onto both with burnt umber.

Carrots—Paint with pumpkin; highlight with mixture of white and pumpkin; shade with mixture of bright red and pumpkin. Dab on leaves using Seminole green, black and yellow and a scruffy brush. Add stems using liner and Seminole green tipped with white.

Radishes—Paint radishes bright red tipped with white. Highlight with a mixture of white and bright red; shade with mixture of bright red and black. Paint leaves Seminole green; highlight with mixture of Seminole green and white; shade with mixture of Seminole green and black and add some bright red.

Turnips—Paint with a mixture of white and purple tipped with white; highlight with a white mixture and shade with purple. Paint leaves Seminole green; highlight with Seminole green mixed with white and shade with Seminole green mixed with black.

Lettuce—Paint head lettuce with a mixture of Seminole green and white. Paint leaf lettuce Seminole green and add bright red for red lettuce and highlight with a mixture of Seminole green, white and bright red. Shade with Seminole green and black. Use Seminole green for other leaf lettuce; highlight with mixture of Seminole green and white and shade with Seminole green and black.

Cucumbers—Paint with Seminole green; shade with mixture of Seminole green and black and highlight with mixture of Seminole green and white. Using toothpick or skewer, add dots of black.

Beets—Paint with a mixture of bright red and purple; add white to mixture for highlighting and add black to mixture for shading. Paint leaves Seminole green and add bright red and purple; highlight with this mixture with some white added and shade with a mixture of black and Seminole green.

Onions—Paint tops Seminole green and bulb white. Shade with black mixture on tops and highlight with white mixture. Shade bulb with mixture of Seminole green and white.

Tomatoes—Paint bright

red; highlight with mixture of bright red, yellow and white; shade with mixture of bright red and black.

Peppers—Paint first pepper yellow; highlight with mixture of white and yellow; shade with mixture of bright red and yellow.

Paint second pepper Seminole green; highlight with mixture of Seminole green and white and shade with mixture of Seminole green and black. Paint chili peppers bright red; highlight with mixture of bright red and yellow;

shade with mixture of bright red and black.

5. Using liner and white paint, add lettering to signs, adding dots to ends of lines in letters with tip of brush handle dipped in white paint. Add directional arrows as desired.

Dry thoroughly.

6. Coat each marker on all surfaces with two coats of gloss exterior varnish.

7. Nail completed markers to post(s) in garden, pointing in direction(s) of vegetables. ✿

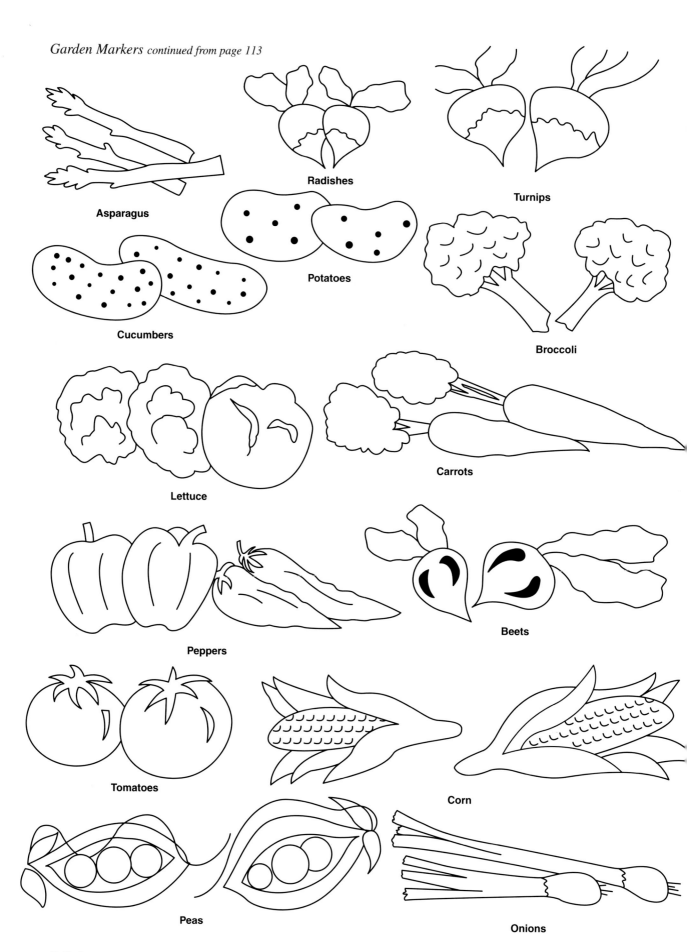

Asparagus

Radishes

Turnips

Cucumbers

Potatoes

Broccoli

Lettuce

Carrots

Peppers

Beets

Tomatoes

Corn

Peas

Onions

Peppery Shakers

Turn bargain-basement salt and pepper shakers into designer originals with a few strokes of the paintbrush! And make sure your bazaar customers know that these shakers can be used for much more than plain old salt and pepper. How about lemon pepper, seasoned salt, and those salt-free herbal seasonings?

Design by Nancy Marshall

Let's Begin!

Materials
Each Pair

- ☐ 2 plain glass salt/pepper shakers
- ☐ Air-Dry PermEnamel Surface Conditioner #45852 and Clear Gloss Glaze #45831 from Delta
- ☐ Air-Dry PermEnamel Paints from Delta: citrus yellow #45005, apple candy green #45023, ultra white #45029 and fire red #45040
- ☐ 2 sponge applicators
- ☐ #5 round paintbrush
- ☐ Toothpick or stylus

Project Notes

Refer to photo and painting diagrams throughout.

Refer to manufacturer's instructions for using Air-Dry PermEnamel products.

Instructions

1. Using sponge applicator, apply conditioner to outside of clean, dry shakers. Let dry and proceed to next step within 4 hours.

2. Paint red peppers on opposite sides of one shaker, painting one color at a time, and letting paint dry between coats. (Two lighter coats are better than one thick coat.)

3. Paint yellow peppers on opposite sides of second shaker.

4. Using tip of toothpick or stylus dipped in paint, dot spots pattern onto unpainted sides, using red and green on shaker with red peppers, and yellow and green on shaker with yellow peppers. ✽

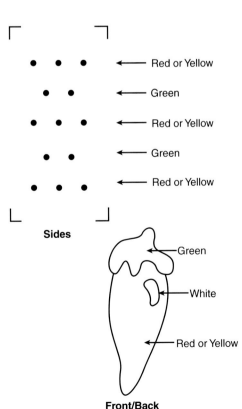

← Red or Yellow
← Green
← Red or Yellow
← Green
← Red or Yellow

Sides

Green
White
Red or Yellow

Front/Back

Starfish & Fish Bowl Magnets

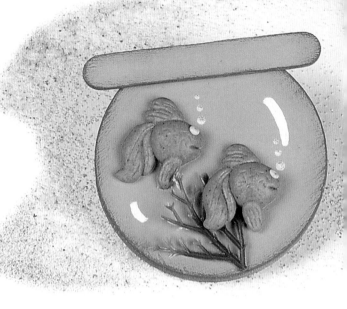

There's something fishy going on here! A pair of magnets starts out as ordinary wooden cutouts, but with the addition of ready-made goldfish and crabs, they take on a decidedly seafaring touch!

Designs by Mary Ayres

Let's Begin!

Materials
Both Magnets

- Wooden pieces from Lara's Crafts: 2½" circle and 3" star
- Forster Craft Stick Mini
- Seaside Crafters Edition Bitty Buddies: 2 goldfish and 2 crabs
- Plastic seaweed
- Americana acrylic paints from DecoArt: white wash #DA2, Salem blue #DA43, sable brown #DA61, sapphire #DA99, light cinnamon #DA114 and honey brown #DA163
- Shimmering silver #DA70 Dazzling Metallics paint from DecoArt
- Paintbrushes: #6 and #8 round bristle brushes and #3 soft round
- ZIG twin-tip black permanent marker from EK Success Ltd.
- White tacky glue
- 2 (2") pieces strip magnet

Project Notes

Refer to photo and patterns throughout.

Refer to directions for dry-brushing under "Painting Techniques" in General Instructions on page 191.

Fish Bowl

1. Paint wooden circle and craft stick mini Salem blue; dry-brush edges with sapphire.

2. Glue craft stick mini across top of circle to make rim of fishbowl. Cut a tiny piece of greenery and glue to bottom front of bowl; glue fish to bowl.

3. Paint three "bubbles" of shimmering silver in a straight vertical line rising from each fish's mouth; bubbles should become gradually smaller as they rise. Add highlight strokes to fish bowl with white wash.

4. Attach one piece of strip magnet to back of magnet.

Starfish

1. Paint wooden star sable brown; dry-brush edges with light cinnamon.

2. Draw solid lines on star with marker's fine tip; add dotted lines with bullet tip.

3. Using tip of paintbrush handle dipped in honey brown, fill each section of starfish with dots of paint.

4. Cut a tiny piece of greenery and glue to starfish; glue on crabs.

5. Attach one piece of strip magnet to back of magnet. ❀

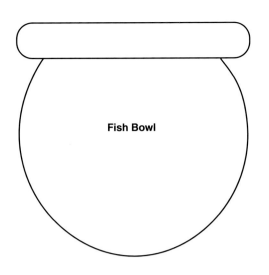

Fish Bowl

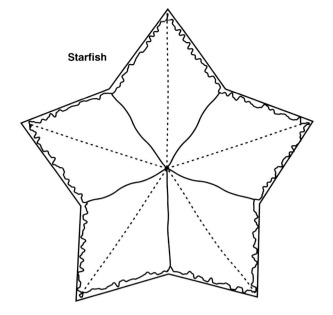

Starfish

Seashell Votives

These diminutive candles are easy to whip up from inexpensive materials. They'll add a romantic and fragrant touch to the powder room, light your dinner table beautifully, or cast a magical glow when lined up on the mantel.

Design by Nancy Marshall

Let's Begin!

Materials
Each Votive

- ☐ Clear glass votive candleholder
- ☐ Jute twine
- ☐ Assorted small seashells, starfish, urchin spines, etc.
- ☐ Clear-drying super glue or cement
- ☐ Votive candle
- ☐ Small paintbrush

Project Note
Refer to photo throughout.

Instructions
1. Wrap jute twine around candleholder six or seven times to make a ¾"-wide band of jute; cut so ends are about 1½" apart. Tie an overhand knot in each end and fray ends. Remove jute.

2. Using small paintbrush, paint a ¾"-wide band of glue or cement around candleholder. Beginning at top edge, rewrap candleholder with jute to cover glue. Clamp ends with clothespins to hold them in place for at least 10 minutes. Remove excess glue with toothpicks or a soft cloth.

3. Glue seven to nine starfish, shells, etc., to jute between knots, overlapping them as desired. Lay candleholder on its side so decorations lay flat until glue dries. (A rolled-up dish towel placed on each side will hold candleholder in place.)

4. Insert candle in candleholder. ✿

Summer by the Sea

Re-create your own bit of Americana—and take advantage of the popularity of nautical motifs—by painting this peaceful seaside scene on a ready-made wooden "saw blade."

Design by Sandra Lee

Let's Begin!

- ☐ 8"-diameter round wooden "saw blade"
- ☐ Gray transfer paper
- ☐ Low-tack tape
- ☐ Americana acrylic paints from DecoArt: white #DA1, cadmium yellow #DA10, hi-lite flesh #DA24, Victorian blue #DA39, burnt sienna #DA63, dark chocolate #DA65, lamp black #DA67, slate grey #DA68, raw sienna #DA93, Hauser light green #DA131, Hauser dark green #DA133, graphite #DA161, winter blue #DA190 and blue chiffon #DA193
- ☐ Paintbrushes and tools: #6 and #12 shaders, ½" rake, 6/0 liner and spatter brush

Project Notes

Refer to photo and pattern throughout.

Refer to directions for transferring pattern under "Using Transfer Paper" in General Instructions on page 190.

Refer to directions for shading under "Painting Techniques" in General Instructions.

Instructions

1. Apply winter blue to top ¼–⅓ of saw blade. Blend in blue chiffon to about the midpoint of saw blade. Beginning approximately at midpoint, blend in hi-lite flesh and apply hi-lite flesh to bottom of saw blade; let dry.

2. Transfer lighthouse pattern to saw blade with transfer paper. Apply strips of low-tack tape along sides of lighthouse to maintain straight lines.

3. *Body and top of lighthouse:* Paint lighthouse titanium white, shading sides with graphite. Paint light at top cadmium yellow, shading with burnt sienna. Using #12 shader, add black stripes to lighthouse; using 6/0 liner, add black details.

4. *Brick base:* Tap dark chocolate, then burnt sienna, then titanium white onto area of brick base, taking care not to blend colors completely. Let dry. With liner and slate grey, add mortar lines.

5. *Dunes and ocean:* Re-define tops of dunes with hi-lite flesh. Paint water with Victorian blue, highlighting with white. Shade sand with raw sienna.

6. *Sea oats and gulls:* Using rake brush, paint some sea oats with Hauser dark green and some with raw sienna; highlight with Hauser light green, and tap on tops of sea oats using raw sienna and burnt sienna. Add simple gulls to sky using 6/0 liner brush and titanium white.

7. Spatter finished piece very lightly with dark chocolate and raw sienna. ✿

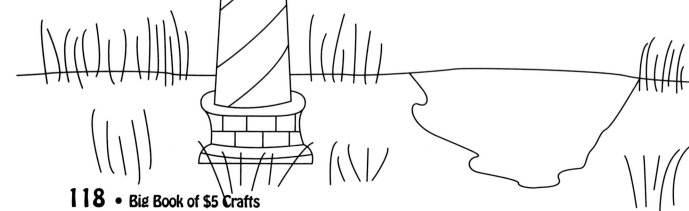

Spring Chick Candle Holder

This little chick is a ready-made candle cup, snuggled in a nest of green excelsior. Pastel paint swirls are an easy way to give the candle a touch of spring, too.

Design by Barbara Mattheissen

Let's Begin!

Materials

- ⅝" wooden candle cup
- Jumbo yellow craft stick from Forster
- 3" terra-cotta flowerpot saucer
- 1½" wooden toy wheel
- Americana acrylic paints from DecoArt: snow white #DA1, cadmium yellow #DA10, cadmium orange #DA14, lamp black #DA67, yellow green #DA134, summer lilac #DA189, and peony pink #DA215
- Paintbrushes: shader, small stencil brush and liner
- DecoArt Candle-Painting medium
- Krylon Crystal Clear spray sealer
- Micron .03 black marking pen
- 6" piece (3mm) pink satin ribbon
- White or off-white taper or carriage candle to fit in candle cup
- Shredded green excelsior
- Craft cement
- Sharp craft snips or craft knife
- Rubbing alcohol
- Waxed paper
- Toothpick

Project Notes

Refer to photo throughout.

Refer to manufacturer's instructions for mixing painting medium with paints.

Allow all paints, ink and sealer to dry between applications.

Chick

1. Paint candle cup cadmium yellow.

2. Referring to Fig. 1, paint chick's facial features on side of candle cup, using stencil brush to paint cheeks peony pink and liner to add orange beak. Add highlights to cheeks using toothpick dipped in white, and add eyes using toothpick dipped in black. Outline beak with black marking pen.

3. Clip both ends from jumbo craft stick, cutting on the diagonal about 1¼" from end. Paint ends cadmium yellow; glue to side of candle cup for wings, points to front and cut edges on top.

4. Following manufacturer's instructions, spray candle cup with sealer.

5. Tie ribbon in a bow; trim ends as desired. Glue to front of chick under beak.

Candle

1. Wipe sides of candle with rubbing alcohol.

2. Mix candle-painting medium with small amounts of peony pink, summer lilac, yellow green and cadmium yellow paints.

3. Pour a puddle of each color ½" apart on one side of a sheet of waxed paper. Draw paintbrush through puddles. Fold plain side of waxed paper over paint puddles and squish paint slightly. Unfold waxed paper.

4. Roll candle across paint mixture so sides are covered. Prop candle in another candle holder to dry.

Finishing

1. Glue toy wheel in center of saucer. Form green excelsior into a ring and glue in saucer around wheel.

2. Glue chick candle cup on top of wheel. Insert candle in cup. ❁

Fig. 1

Tiny Chicklet Candle Holder

Small enough to perch on a cake, this little candle holder made from a wooden spool is a perfect accompaniment to the Spring Chick Candle Holder.

Design by Barbara Matthiessen

Let's Begin!

Materials

- ☐ 1⅛" wooden spool
- ☐ Woodsies wooden products from Forster: medium (1") octagon and large (1½") octagon
- ☐ Americana acrylic paints from DecoArt: snow white #DA1, cadmium yellow #DA10, cadmium orange #DA14, lamp black #DA67, yellow green #DA134 and peony pink #DA215
- ☐ Paintbrushes: shader, small stencil brush and liner
- ☐ Krylon Crystal Clear spray sealer
- ☐ Micron .03 black marking pen
- ☐ Birthday-cake-size candle
- ☐ Craft cement
- ☐ Toothpick

Project Notes

Refer to photo throughout.

Allow all paints, ink and sealer to dry between applications.

Instructions

1. Paint spool cadmium yellow; paint both octagons yellow green.

2. With stencil brush, dab peony pink cheeks on center of side of spool. Using liner, add orange beak. Add highlights to cheeks using toothpick dipped in white, and add eyes using toothpick dipped in black.

3. Using black marking pen, outline beak, add eyebrows and draw tiny lines up from base of spool.

4. Glue medium octagon in center of large one, alternating positions of octagons' points. Center spool atop smaller octagon.

5. Following manufacturer's instructions, spray candle holder with sealer. Insert cake candle. ❁

Lazy Hazy Picnic Bear

Bring on those carefree summer days with this adorable bear figurine.

Design by Charlaine Porter

Let's Begin!

Materials

- ☐ Sculpey III polymer clay: green, white, chocolate, tan, black, light blue, red hot red and yellow
- ☐ 7 black seed beads
- ☐ Small paintbrush
- ☐ Roller
- ☐ Straight pin
- ☐ Wire cutters
- ☐ Needle tool or toothpick
- ☐ Straight-edge tool for cutting and making lines
- ☐ Cookie sheet
- ☐ Parchment paper
- ☐ Oven

Project Note

Refer to photo, pattern and templates (page 123 and 125) throughout.

Instructions

1. *Grass:* Roll 1" ball of green compound; flatten into an oval. Scratch surface with needle tool or toothpick to simulate grass.

2. *Quilt:* Roll ¾" ball of white compound; flatten into a ⅛"-thick square. Set aside. Roll a ⅝" ball of light blue; roll out flat about ⅛" thick and cut ¼"

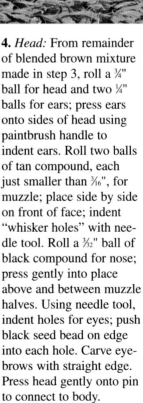

squares for patchwork. Place light blue squares on white square in a checkerboard pattern. Press quilt gently onto grass.

3. *Body:* Thoroughly blend a mixture of one part white and two parts chocolate; roll a 1⅛" ball from mixture. From this ball, pull off enough to make a ⅞" ball of compound; form into body as shown in Fig. 1. Set body on quilt. Cut head off straight pin with wire cutters; push halfway into top of body.

4. *Head:* From remainder of blended brown mixture made in step 3, roll a ¾" ball for head and two ¼" balls for ears; press ears onto sides of head using paintbrush handle to indent ears. Roll two balls of tan compound, each just smaller than ³⁄₁₆", for muzzle; place side by side on front of face; indent "whisker holes" with needle tool. Roll a ³⁄₃₂" ball of black compound for nose; press gently into place above and between muzzle halves. Using needle tool, indent holes for eyes; push black seed bead on edge into each hole. Carve eyebrows with straight edge. Press head gently onto pin to connect to body.

5. *Bow:* Roll ¼" ball of light blue compound; flatten into a 1"-long rope. Flatten rope and cut in half. Cut points in ends for ribbon tails; place on

neck, points down. Roll a ⅜" ball light blue; again roll into 1"-long rope and flatten it; cut in half. Fold each piece in half to make loops; connect ends. Press bow onto bear's neck with paintbrush handle.

6. *Tail:* Roll ⅜" ball from previously blended brown compound; set aside.

7. *Arms and legs:* Roll remaining blended brown mixture into ¼"-thick log; cut into four equal pieces. Shape and press onto body for arms and legs, adjusting as needed if they seem too thick. Attach tail to back of teddy bear.

8. *Watermelon:* Roll ⅜" ball of red hot red compound; flatten into shape of watermelon slice. Mix a little white compound with red hot red to make dark pink; roll into ⅛"-thick rope. Cut a 2"-long piece to fit around red slice. Roll a ⅛"-thick rope of emerald green; cut 2"-long piece and fit around dark pink; flatten and shape to form melon rind. Press black seed bead "seeds" into red portion of watermelon slice; press slice into bear's paws. Make two more "eaten" watermelon rinds with emerald green and dark

pink compound, scratching in "bite marks" with needle tool. Place one rind on quilt and another on grass behind teddy bear.

9. *Sunflowers:* Roll four ³⁄₁₆" balls of yellow compound; flatten slightly. Add small ball of chocolate compound to center of each; poke centers of dots with needle tool. Scallop

edges of yellow flowers with needle tool. Press one sunflower onto teddy bear's head; scatter others on quilt.

10. Set completed piece on a piece of parchment paper on cookie sheet. Bake as directed by compound manufacturer; let cool. ❁

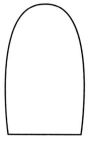

Lazy Hazy Picnic Bear Body

Templates continued on page 125

USA Mini Candle Holder

A special birthday party deserves special candles—and what is your Fourth of July celebration if not a very special birthday party? This project is a great way to add red, white and blue to your Independence Day cookout.

Design by Barbara Matthiessen

Let's Begin!

Materials

- ☐ Wooden products from Woodworks: 1¼" block #SQ-1250 and 3 (¾") spools #SP-6000
- ☐ Americana acrylic paints from DecoArt: snow white #DA1, ultra deep blue #DA100 and Santa red #DA170
- ☐ Antiquing medium
- ☐ Paintbrush
- ☐ .05 Micron Pigma black marking pen
- ☐ Craft glue
- ☐ Small flat buttons: 1 red, 1 blue
- ☐ Narrow jute twine
- ☐ 3 white birthday candles
- ☐ Sandpaper

Project Notes

Refer to photo throughout.

Refer to manufacturer's instructions for applying antiquing medium.

Instructions

1. Paint one spool and the top plus two opposite sides of block with snow white. Paint one spool and the bottom plus one side of block with ultra deep blue. Paint remaining spool and unpainted side of block Santa red. Let dry.

2. Lightly sand spools and edges of blocks to remove some paint for an aged and weathered appearance.

3. Using marker, draw outlines and tiny hash marks around edge of each side of block. Starting with white block, print "U" on one side, "S" on red side and "A" on last white block side.

4. Apply antiquing medium to block and spools; allow medium to dry.

5. Glue spools on top of block in a cluster. Wrap jute twine around cluster and tie in a bow. Glue buttons to bow, overlapping them slightly. Place candles. ❁

Punched Tin Flamingo

Set the tone for summer fun with this simple painted ornament for the window, patio or cabana!

Design by Sandra Graham Smith

Let's Begin!

Materials

- 7" x 8" piece aluminum flashing (see Project Notes)
- Tin snips
- Glossy enamel paints: black, white and hot pink
- Small artist paintbrush
- Pressed-wood board or other hard, protective surface
- Hammer
- Several finishing nails
- Larger nail
- Tracing paper
- Masking tape
- 2 (12") pieces thin wire
- Needle-nose pliers

Project Notes

Refer to photo and patterns throughout.

Aluminum flashing is widely available at hardware stores.

Allow paints to dry between applications of different colors.

Instructions

1. Trace pattern onto tracing paper. Cut out. Tape pattern in place on aluminum flashing; cut out shapes with tin snips.

2. Place tin on protective surface. Use hammer to tap nail from dot to dot, piercing tin. Change nail when point dulls. Make larger holes where indicated using larger nail.

3. Hold up punched tin to light; repunch any holes where necessary. Remove pattern and tape. Smooth side will be back.

4. Paint designs inside punched lines using thick strokes: *white*—eyeball, base of beak and boot cuffs; *hot pink*—flamingo; *black*—beak tip, wing line and boots.

5. Using black and small brush, outline eye and add dot in center; add line and nostril to beak.

6. *Hanger:* Curl 12" piece of wire around pencil; slide off pencil and thread ends through holes in top of flamingo; twist ends to hold hanger in place.

7. *Legs:* Cut remaining piece of wire in half; coil around pencil. Thread one end through holes in bottom of flamingo; twist ends with pliers to hold in place. Thread other end through hole in boots; twist with pliers. ❀

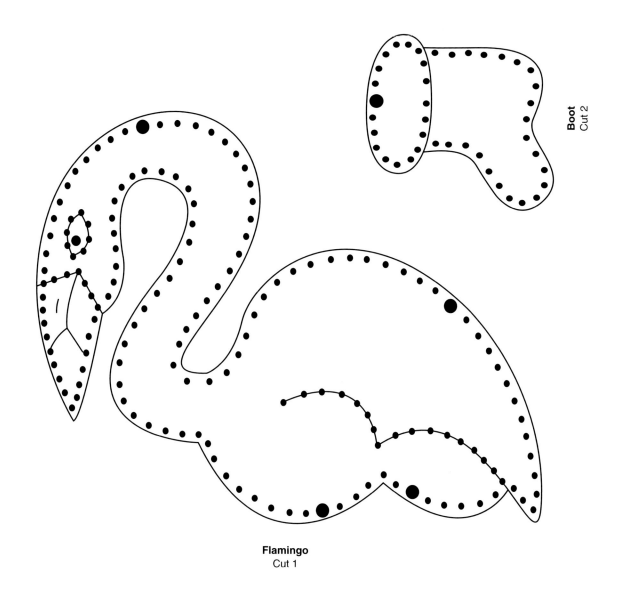

Boot
Cut 2

Flamingo
Cut 1

Lazy Hazy Picnic Bear continued from page 123

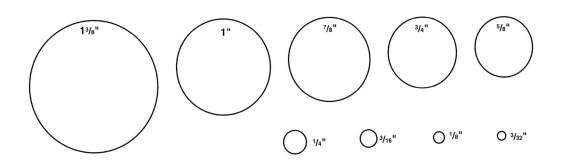

1³/₈"

1"

⁷/₈"

³/₄"

⁵/₈"

¹/₄"

³/₁₆"

¹/₈"

³/₃₂"

Templates for Lazy Hazy Picnic Bear

Fun & Funky Note Minders

These are loads of fun on the kitchen counter or desk. Use them to keep track of notes, tickets, special snapshots, you name it!

Designs by Barbara Matthiessen

Project Notes

Refer to photo throughout. Follow general instructions as given below, painting as directed for individual design.

Let all paints, ink and finish dry between applications.

Instructions

1. Cut flowerpot or latte mug shape from wood. Drill five holes evenly spaced into top edge of flowerpot; drill three holes into latte mug. Sand all rough edges.

2. Paint design:

Flowerpots: Paint all surfaces terra cotta. Dip stencil brush in nutmeg brown; wipe off most paint onto paper towel. Rub down one side of pot and under rim to create shading. Continue rubbing paint down into center of pot. Dab additional nutmeg brown paint across top edge of pot.

Flowers: Using wooden end of paintbrush handle dipped in white, apply five dots of white paint close together; add yellow dot in center. Add stems and leaves with green and liner brush. Add details and squiggly outline with black marker.

"Old Friend": Add lettering and squiggly outline

with black marker.

Latte Mug: Paint all surfaces blue plum. Paint inside of handle outline black. Using wooden end of paintbrush handle dipped in orange, dot a row of dots across top of mug and another across bottom. Using a smaller paintbrush handle dipped in spring green, add rows of dots below orange dots. Using toothpick dipped in black, add dots atop orange dots. Add lettering and outline with black marker.

3. Apply two coats of acrylic finish to design as directed by manufacturer.

4. Cut wires:

Flowers Flowerpot: From copper wire, cut one 11" piece, two 9" and two 6" pieces.

"Friends Flowerpot": From black wire, cut one 9" piece, three 8" pieces and two 5" pieces.

Latte Mug: From black wire, cut one 10" piece and two 7" pieces.

5. Form spiral in one end of each piece by gripping wire with pliers and twisting it into a circle shape. Use pliers to help form the first few rounds, then use your fingers to shape spirals. Form kinks and

Let's Begin!

Materials
Each Note Minder

- ☐ 3½" x 4" piece (¾"-thick) pine stock
- ☐ Micron Pigma 05 black marker
- ☐ Clear acrylic finish
- ☐ Paintbrushes: stencil brush, wash or glaze brush, liner
- ☐ Toothpicks
- ☐ Craft cement
- ☐ Craft saw
- ☐ Craft drill with ⁵⁄₆₄" bit
- ☐ Needle-nose pliers
- ☐ Wire cutters
- ☐ Sandpaper

Flowers Flowerpot

- ☐ Apple Barrel Colors from Plaid: terra cotta, nutmeg brown, white, yellow and spring green
- ☐ 3 feet of 18-gauge copper wire

Friends Flowerpot

- ☐ Apple Barrel Colors from Plaid: terra cotta and nutmeg brown
- ☐ 3 feet of 18-gauge black wire

Latte Mug

- ☐ Apple Barrel Colors from Plaid: blue plum, orange, spring green and black
- ☐ 3 feet of 18-gauge black wire

zigzags in remaining wire as shown or as desired.

6. Dip straight ends of wires into craft cement and insert into holes, placing tallest wire in center and progressively shorter wires in outer holes. (In Friends Flowerpot, place both the longest wire and one of the mid-size wires in center hole.) ❧

Flowers

Flowerpot

Coffee Mug

Straight-Talkin' Signs

Insert your tongue firmly in your cheek, and have a ball painting and selling these fun-loving signs.

Designs by Barbara Matthiessen

Let's Begin!

Materials
Both Signs
- 2 (2¹³⁄₁₆" x 7¼") wooden slats from Forster
- Acrylic paints: white, red and black
- Buttons: 1" red button, plus 7 assorted novelty buttons
- Assorted red and black beads
- Black medium- and fine-point permanent markers
- Paintbrushes: wash brush, stencil brush, and spatter brush or old toothbrush
- Jute twine
- Craft drill with ¹⁄₁₆" bit
- Sandpaper
- Craft snips

Project Notes
Refer to photo and patterns throughout.

See instructions for transferring lettering in General Instructions on page 191.

Let paints and ink dry between applications.

Instructions
1. Drill holes for hangers in two upper corners of each slat.

2. Dip wash brush in water, then into white paint. "Wash" slats with diluted paint.

3. Transfer lettering to sign; trace over lettering with medium marker, adding dots to ends of letters if desired. Add borders on signs with fine-point marker.

4. Finish as directed for individual designs.

Service
1. Thin black paint with water to the consistency of ink. Dip spatter brush in mixture and flick bristles with fingers to spatter sign. Repeat, using red paint.

2. Cut shank off red button and glue to slat.

3. Cut 12" piece of jute; thread beads onto jute and tie knots here and there. Run ends of jute through holes in slat; knot ends to hold hanger in place.

Joy
1. Cut shanks off novelty buttons and glue to sign.

2. Cut 12" piece of jute; thread ends through holes in sign and tie overhand knots in ends. Grasp center of jute hanger and tie an overhand knot about 1½" down. Cut two shorter strands of jute and tie around the hanger in a bow. ❁

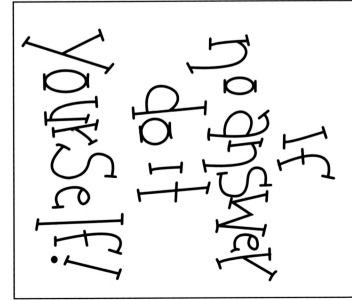

everyone
brings joy
to this
house

some when
they enter
↓

some when
they leave
↑

Kittycat Necklace

Fluffy kittycats in soft pastels are fun to make with pompom "beads." The design works nicely as a lapel pin, too; just glue on a pin back.

Design by Kathy Wegner

Let's Begin!

Materials
Each Necklace

- ☐ Aldastar Pom Beadz in desired color: 1 (1½"), 1 (1") and 2 (½")
- ☐ 1 yard matching (⅛"-wide) satin ribbon
- ☐ Craft foam: scrap of light pink and ¾" x 1½" strip to match pompom beads
- ☐ 2 (3mm) round black wiggle eyes
- ☐ White embroidery floss
- ☐ White tacky glue
- ☐ Large-eye needle

Project Note
Refer to photo and pattern throughout.

Instructions
1. Cut a ¼"-wide triangle from light pink craft foam for nose; from color that matches pompom beads, cut one pair of ears.

2. Thread ½" pompom beads (feet) onto ribbon; push to center of ribbon. Thread both ribbon ends through needle and thread needle through 1½" pompom bead (body), then 1" pompom bead (head). Push pompom beads together snugly, securing them with dots of glue.

3. *Whiskers:* Cut two single plies of white floss 2" long. Glue eyes and whiskers onto cat's head, then glue nose over center of whiskers. Let dry.

4. Knot ribbon ends to desired length. Apply glue to base of ears; press down into top of cat's head just behind ribbon. ❀

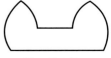

Kitty Cat Ears
Cut 1 from craft foam

Crazy Creatures

Stand them on a dresser, perch them on your windowsill, glue them to spring clothespins to secure notes ... their uses are endless! Have a ball concocting a whole herd of whimsical critters!

Designs by Barbara Woolley

Project Notes

Refer to photo, Fig. 1 and pattern throughout.

Craft foam can be painted if desired.

Instructions

1. Dab desired color of paint over foam ball using a small piece of sponge; let dry.

2. Using another piece of sponge, paint gingerbread men (feet), squares (beak) and mini sticks (legs) yellow. (If using clothespin, omit mini sticks and paint clothespin yellow or to match body.)

3. Drill hole in center of each foot; glue one end of mini stick in each (gingerbread man's head will be back of foot). Take care so

that bottom surface of foot is flat. Glue other ends of stick legs into foam ball body. (If using clothespin, omit drilling step; glue feet to bottom of foam ball and glue clothespin to bottom of feet.)

4. Apply glue to one corner of each painted wooden square and insert points into foam, pressing about half of each square into foam to form top and bottom of beak. Glue eyes in place.

5. Cut wire in half; coil around pencil. Slide coiled wire off pencil and glue to top of foam ball for antennae.

6. Referring to Fig. 1, glue three yellow feathers into foam ball and surround with feathers of other color(s).

7. Cut two arms from craft foam; glue to creature. ❀

Let's Begin!

Materials
Each Creature

- 2" plastic foam ball
- Craft glue
- 2 (⅜") round glass or acrylic eyes in color of your choice
- Woodsies wooden cutouts from Forster: 2 medium gingerbread men, 2 small squares and 2 mini sticks
- Wooden spring-type clothespin (optional)
- 2" x ½" strip craft foam in color of your choice
- 5" piece yellow covered wire or yellow chenille stem
- Feathers: 3 (2") yellow and 16 (2") in assorted/desired colors
- Acrylic paints: yellow plus color of your choice
- Small pieces of sponge to apply paint
- Craft drill with bit to match diameter of mini sticks

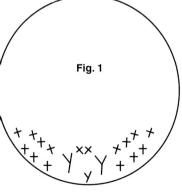

Fig. 1

Feather Placement
Y = yellow feather
X = other color feather

Crazy Creatures Arms
Cut 2 from craft foam

Witch Doll Pin

From her bright green nose to her orange hair and tiny broom, this little sorceress casts a spell of lighthearted fun. Wear one on your jumper or lapel and watch smiles appear like magic!

Design by Mary Ayres

Let's Begin!

Materials

- 1" x 1" natural extra-small round knit bag from Wimpole Street Creations
- Small natural long skin from Wimpole Street Creations
- Olive green #DA56 Americana acrylic paint from DecoArt
- Fabric cut with pinking shears: 2" x 5" purple Halloween print, 1¾" x 5" black satin, and 1" x 3" black felt
- 6-strand embroidery floss: light orange and dark orange
- ½" flat gold star button
- 2 (3mm) wiggle eyes
- 5mm light green pompom
- 4" piece (⅛"-wide) purple satin ribbon
- ¼ yard (¼"-wide) metallic green ribbon
- 2" straw broom
- 1½" gold pin back
- Small bowl
- Polyester fiberfill
- Tacky craft glue
- Pinking shears
- Hand-sewing needle and matching threads
- 2 knitting needles or other pointed objects

Project Note

Refer to photo throughout.

Instructions

1. In small bowl, mix one capful of paint and two capfuls of water. Saturate small knit bag (head) and long skin (body) in mixture; wring excess paint mixture from pieces and let them air-dry by suspending them from the points of knitting needles that are standing in a glass. (If pieces dry flat, the back side turns a darker color.)

2. Fill head and body with fiberfill using knitting needles to push fiberfill into ends of arms and legs. Glue head opening inside body opening. Let dry.

3. *Dress:* For armholes, cut 1" slit along one long edge of pinked purple print rectangle 1¼" from each side. Fold rectangle in half widthwise, right sides facing, and sew short sides together ¼" from edge. Turn right side out. Sew basting stitch close to neck edge, joining armholes as you work your way around. Put dress on witch. Gather basting stitches tightly around neck and knot to secure.

4. *Hair:* Separate light orange and dark orange floss into 3-strand pieces, and cut 10 (4") pieces of each color. Lay floss together in a bunch with ends even. Tie in center with a 6" piece of light orange floss. Glue hair across top of head with knot in center. Trim floss ends even and separate strands.

5. *Hat:* Wrap and glue felt rectangle around head, overlapping short ends in the back and forming a point at the top of the hat. Glue purple ribbon around hat ¼" from bottom edge with ends in back. Glue star button to right front side of hat on top of purple hatband.

6. *Cape:* Sew basting stitch along one long side of black satin 1¾" x 5" rectangle close to the edge. Pull stitches tightly to gather cape so it measures 1½" across gathered edge. Knot thread ends to secure; glue gathered edge of cape to back of witch under hat.

7. *Face:* Glue pompom to center of face for nose; glue eyes above nose so that they touch.

8. Tie green ribbon in a tiny bow; trim ends even. Glue bow to center top of dress. Glue broom to dress front so it looks like witch is holding broom handle. Let dry. Glue pin back vertically to center back of hat and cape. Let dry. ✿

Mr. Bones

Meet Mr. Bones, the ... er ... life of any Halloween party! Easily made from wooden craft sticks, he'll dance and jig his way into your guests' hearts—even though he seems to have lost his somewhere.

Design by Kathy Wegner

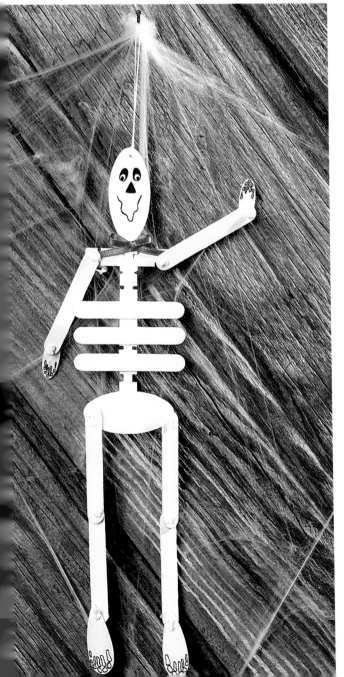

Materials

- ☐ Wooden products from Forster: 2 large Woodsies (2"-long) ovals, 2 medium Woodsies (1½"-long) teardrops, 2 small Woodsies (1"-long) ovals, 2 Skill Sticks and 9 craft stick minis
- ☐ White acrylic paint
- ☐ Paintbrush
- ☐ Matte varnish
- ☐ Black fine-line permanent marking pen
- ☐ 24" piece white string
- ☐ 12" piece white elastic thread
- ☐ Large-eye needle
- ☐ 8" piece (¼"-wide) orange satin ribbon
- ☐ Craft drill with ¹⁄₁₆" bit
- ☐ Wood glue

Project Notes

Refer to photo throughout.

Lay wood pieces on top of a piece of smooth, flat scrap wood to stabilize them when drilling holes.

Let paints and ink dry between coats and before applying ink and varnish.

Test varnish with marker; some markers may run. Thinned black acrylic paint applied with a liner brush may be substituted for the marking pen.

Instructions

1. Break both 1¼" ends off one Skill Stick, keeping 2" center. On skeleton's spine (whole Skill Stick), glue large ovals for head and hipbone; glue 2" Skill Stick section below head and behind spine to make shoulders. Glue three craft stick minis above hipbone for ribs; let dry.

2. *Drill holes:* Drill a hole in both ends of six craft stick minis still unattached;

these are arms and legs. Drill hole in pointed ends of medium teardrops; drill hole in one end of small ovals; drill holes in both ends of shoulders and hip-bones; drill hole through head at top.

3. Paint all surfaces with white paint; add a second coat if needed. Using marking pen, draw face, finger bones and toe bones. Coat all pieces with one or two coats matte varnish.

4. Thread needle with string. Attach wood pieces to each other by knotting string, pulling through holes in pieces to be joined, and knotting string again close to wood; trim excess. Repeat until Mr. Bones is complete.

5. Thread elastic through hole in head; knot to make hanging loop.

6. Tie ribbon in a bow around Mr. Bones' neck; trim excess ribbon. ❁

Pumpkin Garland

Drape a string of these jack-o'-lanterns with silly faces along the walls or in the doorway for Halloween—and watch the smiles appear! Who would guess that the "pumpkins" are really light bulbs?

Design by Bev Shenefield

Let's Begin!

Materials

- 3 vanity-type round light bulbs
- 3 (⅜"-diameter) wooden furniture plugs
- 60" piece soft jute twine
- Silk maple leaves or other leaves
- Craft cement
- CeramDecor PermEnamel paints from Delta: chocolate #45004, tangerine #45008, burnt sienna #45010, ultra white #45029, red red #45033 and ultra black #45034
- Ceramcoat surface conditioner and clear satin glaze from Delta
- Paintbrushes: size ¾ filbert, ¹⁰⁄₀ liner, size 4 spotting and old scruffy paintbrush

Project Note

Refer to photo and patterns for pumpkin faces throughout.

Instructions

1. Wash light bulbs; dry thoroughly. Apply surface conditioner with filbert brush.

2. Using filbert, paint bulbs with tangerine. Let dry one hour and apply a second coat. Apply a third coat if needed to cover completely.

3. Trace patterns of faces onto bulbs. Paint eyes and teeth ultra white; paint mouth and outline teeth using liner and ultra black. Paint pupils ultra black with spotting brush. Highlight with ultra white and liner.

4. Paint plugs tangerine on front only; highlight with ultra white. Using scruffy brush, dab red red on cheeks.

5. Seal painted surfaces with clear satin glaze.

6. Cement plugs in place for noses, making sure highlight is on top.

7. Paint bases of light bulbs chocolate; streak with burnt sienna. Apply two coats if necessary to cover; let dry completely.

8. Apply cement to base of bulb. Beginning 12" from one end of jute, wrap around base from both sides. Repeat on other end. When both are dry enough to handle without bulbs falling off, wind center of jute around base of third bulb in same manner.

9. Glue leaves around bases of bulbs. ✿

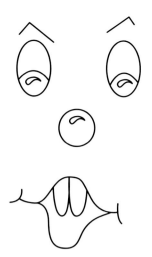

Pumpkin Garland Faces

Black Cat Pin

This pretty kitty is easy to make with precut wooden shapes and a few touches of paint.

Design by Bev Shenefield

Let's Begin!

Materials

- Woodsies wooden cutouts from Forster: 2" (large) oval, 1" (small) heart, ⅞" (small) oval, and 2" (medium) teardrop
- Craft cement
- Toothpick, pin or pencil
- 1" pin back
- CeramDecor PermEnamel paints from Delta: ultra white #45029, red red #45033, ultra black #45034 and limeade #45126
- Ceramcoat clear gloss glaze from Delta (optional)
- Paintbrushes: size ¾ filbert, size 10/0 script liner and size 8 flat

Project Notes

Refer to photo and pattern throughout.
Let cement and paints dry between applications.

Instructions

1. Cement heart (head) near center of large oval (body) with point of heart pointing up; cement teardrop (tail) to back of large oval at top with pointed end up. Glue small oval (paws) across bottom of body on wrong side.

2. Paint cat on all surfaces with ultra black.

3. Blend red red with ultra white to make pink. Using liner, paint ears, nose and tongue with mixture.

4. Dip tip of paintbrush handle into limeade; dot on eyes. When dry, dot on tiny, tiny pupils of ultra black using the very fine tip of a toothpick, pin or pencil. Add whiskers and claws using liner brush and ultra white.

5. Coat painted cat with

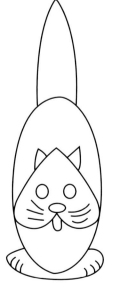

Black Cat Pin

glaze if desired. Cement pin back onto back. ❀

Spooky Smiles Mug & Trivet

This great gift idea features a mug painted to look like candy corn and a coordinating mug rest featuring a bat on a simple ceramic trivet.

Designs by Annie Lang

Let's Begin!

Materials
Each Project
- ☐ Transfer paper
- ☐ Ultra-Gloss Air Dry enamel paints from DecoArt: white #DG1, black #DG2, butter milk #DG3, lemon yellow #DG5, cadmium yellow #DG6, orange #DG7 and Christmas red #DG10
- ☐ Paintbrushes: #5 and #10 pointed rounds, and size 1 liner (optional)

Mug
- ☐ White or off-white ceramic mug
- ☐ 1" square cut from household sponge

Trivet
- ☐ 4" square white ceramic tile
- ☐ 4" square black felt
- ☐ Craft glue

Project Notes
Refer to photo and patterns throughout.

Refer to directions for transferring pattern under "Using Transfer Paper" in General Instructions on page 191.

Refer to paint manufacturer's instructions for washing painted pieces.

Mug
1. Wash mug in soapy water; rinse well and dry thoroughly.

2. Paint mug by sponging bands of color, each approximately 1" wide, up from base, graduating colors until you reach the rim. To sponge on color, dampen sponge and wring out until it is almost dry. Dip sponge into paint and pounce it up and down on palette a few times to work paint into the sponge. Then gently pounce color up and down on surface.

3. Starting at base, sponge a line of orange around mug. While orange is still a little wet, sponge a line of cadmium yellow along top edge of orange. If you overlap the orange slightly, the colors will gently blend together. In same manner, add a band of lemon yellow above cadmium yellow; near top edge of mug, add a band of buttermilk so it blends gently with lemon yellow. Let dry.

Spooky Smiles Mug

Spooky Smiles Trivet

4. Using #10 round brush, paint entire handle black.

5. Transfer face pattern onto opposite sides of mug. Using #10 round brush, tap some Christmas red onto cheeks; paint nose with Christmas red using #5 round brush.

Using liner and black, add eyes, mouth and detail lines. When dry, add tiny white highlight dots to nose, cheeks and eyes with liner.

Trivet

1. Wash ceramic tile in soapy water; rinse well and dry thoroughly.

2. Transfer bat pattern to center of tile. Using #10 round brush, paint bat black. When dry, use #5 round to fill in whites of eyes and add orange bow tie. Using liner, add white highlight lines to face, body and wings. Using liner, paint black eye pupils, "movement" lines and bow tie details.

3. Glue felt square to bottom of trivet. ❁

Mini Felt Treat Bags

These little sacks are easy to whip up with pre-stiffened felt, and fun to fill with treats. A basketful will make a super addition to your autumn bazaar table.

Designs by Nancy Marshall

Let's Begin!

Materials
Both Bags

- ☐ 12" x 18" sheets CPE Eazy Felt stiffened felt: black and white
- ☐ 9" chenille stems: 2 orange and 2 black
- ☐ 4 (7mm) round black wiggle eyes
- ☐ 2 (9") pieces (⅛"-wide) orange satin ribbon
- ☐ ¼" round paper punch
- ☐ Fabric-paint markers: black and white
- ☐ Tacky craft glue
- ☐ Iron (optional)

Project Note
Refer to photo, Fig. 1 and patterns throughout.

Instructions
1. Cut one bag from each color felt; cut also one ghost from white and one bat from black.

2. *Assemble bag:* Fold along dotted lines, pressing folds with warm iron if desired. Apply glue to right side of tabs, then press to wrong side of bag front and back. Let dry.

3. Punch holes for handles in front and back of bags.

Bend orange chenille stem into handle shape; insert ends through holes on front of black bag. Twist ends around stems to secure handle. Repeat with remaining orange chenille stem on black bag, and black stems on white bag.

4. Glue eyes to bat and ghost; add smiles with white and black paint markers. Tie each piece of ribbon into a small bow; glue one to front of each character.

5. Glue bat to front of white bag and ghost to front of black bag. ❈

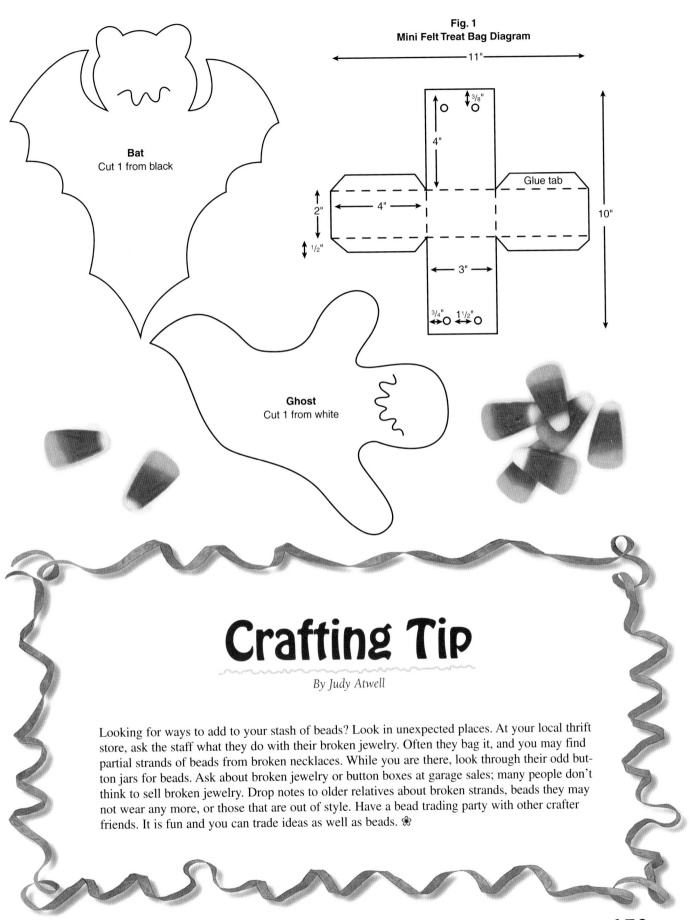

Bat
Cut 1 from black

Ghost
Cut 1 from white

Fig. 1
Mini Felt Treat Bag Diagram

11"

3/8"

4"

Glue tab

2"

4"

10"

1/2"

3"

3/4" 1 1/2"

Crafting Tip

By Judy Atwell

Looking for ways to add to your stash of beads? Look in unexpected places. At your local thrift store, ask the staff what they do with their broken jewelry. Often they bag it, and you may find partial strands of beads from broken necklaces. While you are there, look through their odd button jars for beads. Ask about broken jewelry or button boxes at garage sales; many people don't think to sell broken jewelry. Drop notes to older relatives about broken strands, beads they may not wear any more, or those that are out of style. Have a bead trading party with other crafter friends. It is fun and you can trade ideas as well as beads. ✤

Mini Papier-Mâché Gift Boxes

Decorative scrapbook papers dress up the lids of tiny boxes to make perfect containers for little gifts and treats. They'll dress up place settings on your fall table, too!

Design by Nancy Marshall

Let's Begin!

Materials
Each Box

☐ 2½" square papier-mâché box with lid

☐ 5" square of decorative scrapbook paper (see Project Notes)

☐ Peel n Stick double-sided adhesive sheets from Therm O Web

☐ Approximately 20" (¼"-wide) gold-and-dark-green Raffia Accents ribbon from Plaid Enterprises

☐ Tacky craft glue

Project Notes

Sample projects were made using Paper Pizzazz scrapbook papers in Candy Corn and Autumn Leaves designs from Hot Off the Press. Each sheet of scrapbook paper will make two box lids.

Refer to photo and pattern throughout.

Instructions

1. Cut 4⅝" square of

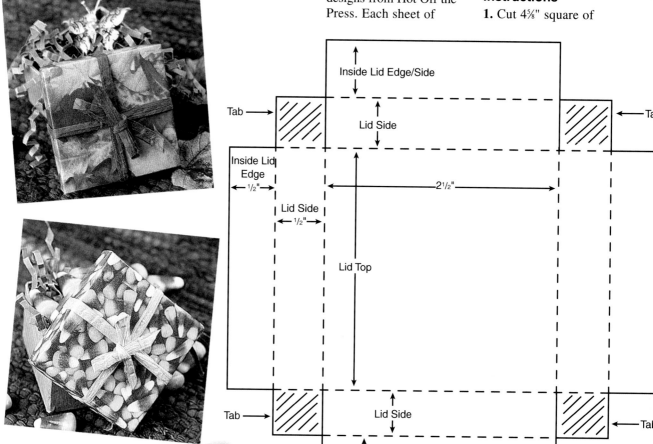

Mini Papier-Mâché Gift Boxes
Cut along solid lines;
fold on dashed lines

adhesive. Peel backing from one side only and adhere to wrong side of scrapbook paper. Transfer pattern for box lid to paper backing on adhesive; cut lid from scrapbook paper.

2. Carefully peel backing from scrapbook paper lid. Lay paper adhesive side up on work surface. Center papier-mâché lid on it. Fold up two side sections with tabs, folding tabs to adjacent sides, and continue to fold paper to inside of lid.

Fold remaining sides to finish covering lid. If desired, cut a square of decorative paper to fit inside lid and affix with glue or another piece of adhesive.

3. Cut two pieces of raffia ribbon to fit across lid top, edges and underside (about 5"). Gluing ends, center one piece across lid; repeat with second piece across opposite sides. Cut a 9" piece of raffia ribbon; slide under intersection of pieces and tie in a bow. ❀

Glass Bottle Ladies

Dress up inexpensive miniature bottles to make attractive accents for dresser or bric-a-brac.

Designs by Maggie Rampy

Let's Begin!

Materials
Each Lady
- [ ] 5" glass bottle
- [ ] 1" wooden ball knob with flat bottom
- [ ] 10" piece (1"-wide) white or cream flat lace
- [ ] Matching sewing thread and needle
- [ ] Mini-curl doll hair
- [ ] 2"–2½" straw or lace hat with 1" opening
- [ ] Assorted trims: ⅛" satin ribbon, silk flowers, leaves, etc.
- [ ] Acrylic paints: black and white
- [ ] Powdered cosmetic blusher
- [ ] Paintbrush with ⅛" round wooden handle
- [ ] Toothpick
- [ ] Cotton-tip swab
- [ ] White tacky craft glue
- [ ] Hot-glue gun

Project Note
Refer to photo throughout.

Instructions
1. Using tacky glue, glue flat edge of ball knob to top lip of bottle; let dry.

2. Using your finger, lightly color front half of head with cosmetic blusher.

3. Lightly mark position of eyes with pencil. Dip paintbrush handle in black paint and dot eyes onto face. When paint is dry, dip tip of toothpick into white paint and dot highlight onto upper right side of each eye.

4. Add more blush to cheeks with cotton-tip swab.

5. *Collar:* Overlap ends of lace ½". Using needle and thread, sew running stitch around straight edge. Place collar over lady's head and pull ends of thread to gather it evenly around her neck.

6. Cut hair into 1" lengths. Hot-glue hair to head, beginning on front of head and placing two strands of hair in each small dot of hot glue. Work down sides of face, finish top of head, then cover back of head. Trim hair as desired.

7. Decorate hat as desired, then hot-glue onto lady's head. Add ribbon bow at neckline and other trims as desired. ❀

Holiday Accents

Dress up your home from holiday to holiday with this delightful assortment of crafts for celebrating New Year's Day, Valentine's Day, St. Patrick's Day, Easter, Fourth of July, Halloween, Thanksgiving, Hanukkah and Christmas!

New Year's Hot Plate

This tile trivet holds dishes of hot New Year's treats while adding a stylish touch to your holiday buffet.

Design by June Fiechter

Let's Begin!

Materials

- ☐ 7¾" square white ceramic tile
- ☐ EtchAll products from B&B Etching Products Inc.: Dip 'n Etch and resist gel
- ☐ ZIG Painty Pens from EK Success Ltd.: white and copper
- ☐ Ceramcoat Sparkle Glaze from Delta

Project Notes

Refer to photo and patterns throughout.

Wear rubber gloves when working with etching products, and follow manufacturer's instructions for using them.

Instructions

1. Trace pattern 1 onto center of tile. Apply resist gel over traced pattern.

2. Pour Dip 'n Etch into a square plastic container larger than the tile. Gently submerge tile in Dip 'n Etch liquid. Wait as directed by manufacturer and remove tile.

3. Rinse tile well, removing gel after surface has been completely rinsed.

4. Using pattern 2, embellish etched tile with white and copper pens.

5. Apply sparkle glaze to etched, painted surface. ❀

Pattern 1

Pattern 2

Recycled Candles

Any candle—even one with dings and nicks—can be transformed with a simple application of beads or other crafting goodies.

Design by Beth Wheeler

Let's Begin!

Materials

- ☐ Candle of desired size, shape and color
- ☐ Crafter's Pick Ultimate Tacky Glue by API
- ☐ Beads, pearls or sea glass
- ☐ Plastic spoon
- ☐ Waxed paper

Project Notes

Refer to photo throughout.

Crafter's Pick Ultimate Tacky Glue is recommended for its holding power and thickness. Even glass pieces are held in place without sagging or slipping.

Position any flammable material toward the bottom of the candle only. Stop burning candle at least 1" above the flammable material.

Perking Up Aged Candles

Smooth superficial scratches and dull the finish by rubbing candles with a pair of clean pantyhose.

To add texture, warm wax with a warm—not hot—hair dryer, then roll candle on a piece of screen, sandpaper or other textured surface.

Chop old candles into chunks. Pack them into a candle mold with a new wick and pour new wax on top.

Other Goodies to Glue on Candles

Buttons

Pearls or beads from old jewelry or broken beaded purse

Coffee beans

Cinnamon sticks

Colored paper clips

Small pebbles

Flat-back marbles

Shells

Colored sand

Instructions

1. Apply glue in an uneven band along bottom or down sides of candle; smooth glue with plastic spoon.

2. Sprinkle beads, pearls or sea glass on glue with fingers or plastic spoon.

Press into glue with fingertips to secure.

3. Place candle on a piece of waxed paper and leave undisturbed until glue is completely dry, approximately 24 hours. ❀

Valentine Pin

With the help of precut wooden shapes, it's simple to create this sweet little valentine cherub.

Design by Paula Bales

Let's Begin!

Project Notes

Refer to photo and pattern throughout.

Paint all surfaces of wooden pieces.

Let all paints, ink and varnish dry between applications.

Instructions

1. Paint 1¼" circle berry red for body; dot with pastel pink and white applied with tip of paintbrush handle and the head of a straight pin.

2. Using flesh, paint ¾" circle (head) and both ⅜" circles (hands).

3. Using pastel pink, paint 1" heart; using white, paint 1¼" hearts (wings); add comma-stroke accents of pastel pink at curves of wings.

4. Paint heart and wings with sparkle varnish. When dry, write "Happy Valentines" on small heart and add outline with marking pen.

5. Using head of straight pin, dot black eyes and berry red nose onto head; when dry, highlight eyes with tiny specks of white. Lightly rouge cheeks with berry red.

Materials

- Woodsies wooden cutouts from Forster: 1 each ¾" and 1¼" circle and 1" heart; 2 each ⅜" circles and 1 ¼" hearts
- Apple Barrel acrylic paints from Plaid: berry red #525, pastel pink #783, white #503, flesh #514 and black #504
- FolkArt sparkle varnish from Plaid
- Paintbrushes: #4 shader and 5/0 spotter
- Straight pin
- Black electrical wire
- Wire cutters
- ⅛"-wide pink satin ribbon
- Tacky craft glue
- Hot-glue gun
- Black ultra-fine–point marking pen
- 1" pin back

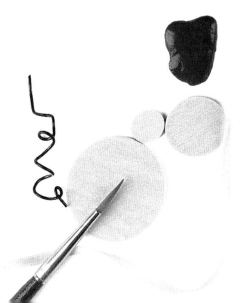

6. Using marker, draw eyelashes, eyebrows and smile; outline head, hands and wings.

7. Glue points of wings to wrong side of body; glue head to top front edge of body. Glue heart to center of body and hands to upper sections of heart.

8. *Hair:* Cut several 1" pieces of wire; curl them around paintbrush handle. Glue ends to wrong side of head; arrange hair as desired.

9. Tie tiny bow from pink ribbon; glue at neckline off to left side. Glue pin back to back of pin. ❧

Valentine Pin

Hugs & Kisses Tic-Tac-Toe

Give an old favorite a romantic spin! Kids of all ages will enjoy playing with this neat self-contained game.

Design by Bev Shenefield

Project Notes

Refer to photo throughout.

Let all coats of paint, ink and varnish dry between applications.

Instructions

1. Using flat brush, paint corrugated sides of box and interior of box and lid with metallic 14K gold paint.

2. Sponge outside of lid and flat edge and bottom of box with Moroccan red; repeat, using raspberry. As you paint, keep turning sponge so no lines are left.

3. Paint five hearts Moroccan red and five raspberry. Sponge edges with metallic 14K gold. Using liner and white paint, paint "HUGS" on each raspberry heart and "KISSES" on each Moroccan red heart.

4. Using chalk pencil, mark a grid for playing tic-tac-toe on box lid; go over lines with fine-line gold pen. When dry, carefully remove chalk lines with dampened paper towel.

5. Using extra-fine-line

Let's Begin!

Materials

- 5½" papier-mâché box with corrugated sides
- 10 (1") wooden hearts with scalloped edges #U10762 from Lara's Crafts
- Marvy fine-line and extra-fine-line Liquid Gold pens
- Chalk pencil
- Cosmetic sponge
- Ceramcoat acrylic paints from Delta: white #2505, raspberry #2520, Moroccan red #2552 and metallic 14K gold #2604
- Gloss interior varnish
- Paintbrushes: #12 flat and 10/0 liner

gold pen, write "TIC TAC TOE" on edge of box lid along one side and "HUGS AND KISSES" on edge along other side of lid.

6. Coat all surfaces of box and playing pieces with two coats varnish. ❀

Valentine Gift Tote & Card

Whip these up in a snap with corrugated paper hearts and buttons.

Designs by Angie Wilhite

Let's Begin!

Materials
Card & Tote

- ☐ Paper Reflections products from DMD Industries: 5" x 7" kraft greeting card and envelope; 8¼" x 5¼" kraft bag; 3 (4") burgundy and 2 (4") white corrugated paper folk hearts; burgundy heart, gold heart and 2 burgundy button stickers; 1 sheet Country Cup burgundy tissue
- ☐ 3 (½") white heart-shaped buttons
- ☐ 6 (½") burgundy round buttons
- ☐ Craft adhesive
- ☐ Deckle-edge paper edgers from Fiskars
- ☐ ZIG Millennium .05 black pigment marker from EK Success Ltd.

Project Note
Refer to photo throughout.

Envelope & Card
1. Trim long edge of envelope flap and open edges on front of card with paper edgers.

2. Affix all stickers to envelope flap.

3. Glue corrugated white heart to front of card; overlap with one burgundy corrugated heart and glue in place.

4. Glue burgundy button at top center of white heart and white button at top center of burgundy heart; glue two more burgundy buttons to kraft surface of card front.

5. Using black marker, outline hearts with broken line.

Gift Tote
1. Glue burgundy corrugated heart to upper third of sack; overlap with white corrugated heart, then overlap white heart with remaining burgundy corrugated heart.

2. Glue white buttons to top center of burgundy hearts; glue burgundy button to top center of white heart; glue remaining burgundy buttons to kraft surface of bag. Using black marker, outline hearts with broken line.

3. Use burgundy tissue to cradle gift in bag. ❀

Green & Gold Shamrock Card

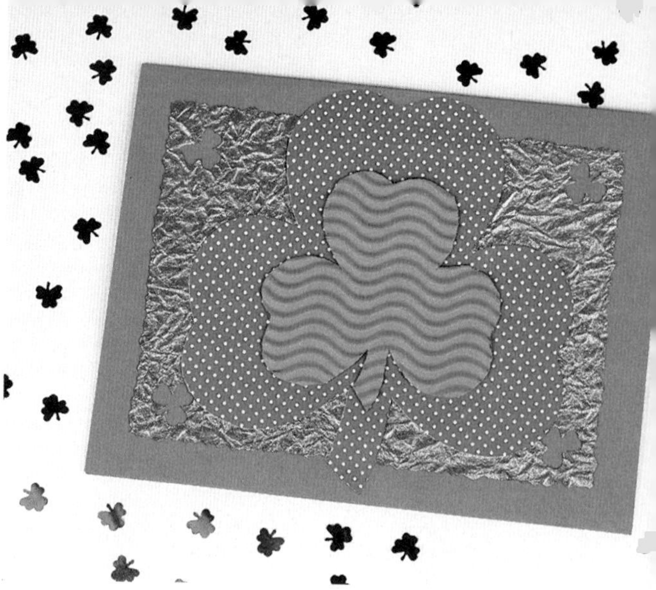

Your greetings bring with them all the luck o' the Irish when they come in this colorful card crafted from scrapbook papers.

Design by Kathy Wegner

Let's Begin!

Materials

- 6½" x 5" blank green greeting card with envelope
- Paper Reflections decorative papers from DMD Industries: 6" x 4½" piece metallic gold, 5½" square green with white pin dots, and 3½" square wavy green corrugated
- Adhesive mounting sheets
- Deckle paper edgers from Fiskars
- Shamrock paper punch (optional)

Project Notes

Refer to photo and patterns throughout.

Follow manufacturer's directions for using adhesive mounting sheets.

Instructions

1. From adhesive mounting sheets cut one piece 6" x 4½", one 5½" square and one 3¼" square. Apply adhesive to backs of gold, green pin-dot and corrugated papers respectively.

2. Trace large shamrock onto wrong side of green-and-white pin-dot paper; trace small shamrock onto wrong side of corrugated green paper; cut out.

3. Trim edges of gold paper with deckle paper edgers; punch a shamrock in each corner if desired.

4. Peel release paper from back of gold paper; press onto front of card. Top with pin-dot shamrock, and then corrugated shamrock. Insert card in envelope. ❀

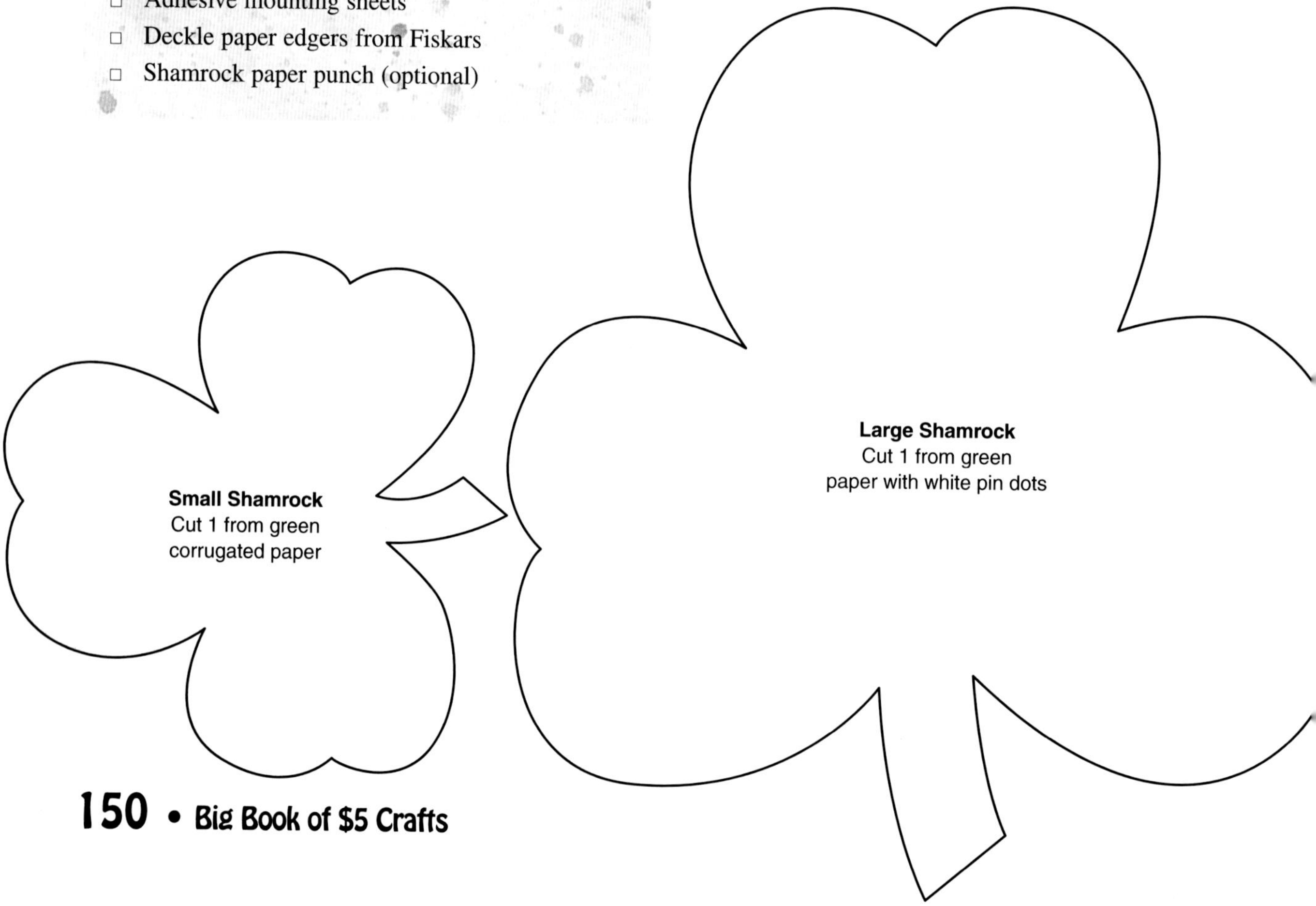

Small Shamrock
Cut 1 from green
corrugated paper

Large Shamrock
Cut 1 from green
paper with white pin dots

St. Pat's Bath Beads

Here's a simple project that can be adapted easily for other holidays and occasions. Give your imagination free rein as you embellish the bottle with paints, ribbon and trims.

Design by June Fiechter

Let's Begin!

Materials

- Empty, clean wine bottle
- Bath salts
- Decorative shamrock
- 16" piece white ribbon
- Kiwi #45-105-0202 Perm Enamel Frosted Looks paint from Delta
- Paintbrush
- White paper for label or computer-printed label

Project Note

Refer to photo throughout.

Instructions

1. Paint bottle with kiwi paint; let dry. Fill bottle with bath salts.

2. Tie ribbon in a bow around neck of bottle; glue shamrock in center of bow.

3. Glue label to bottle. ✿

Have a Lucky Day

Party Favor Mini Pot

Spruce up your holiday table with this colorful little decoration filled with treats of the season.

Designs by Kathy Wegner

Let's Begin!

Materials
- 1½" terra-cotta flowerpot
- Gold #OC 301 Aleene's Premium-Coat acrylic paint from Duncan Enterprises
- Scribbles 3D Shinyt paints from Duncan Enterprises: bright green #SC 134 and lime green #SC 164
- Matte sealer
- Craft foam: lime green and green
- 4 (5") pieces green plastic-coated wire
- 1¼" square gold felt
- Tacky craft glue
- Black fine-point permanent marker
- Small paintbrush
- Toothpick
- Small seasonal treats—jelly beans, etc.

Project Notes
Refer to photo and pattern throughout.

Let all paints, ink and sealer dry between applications.

Instructions
1. Cut four shamrocks each from lime green and green craft foam. Glue to ends of wires in matching pairs, sandwiching ends of wires between shamrocks.

2. Sponge two coats of gold paint over all surfaces of flowerpot.

3. Using small paintbrush and toothpick as needed, decorate pots with small flowers of 3D paints, alternating lime green flowers with bright green centers and bright green flowers with lime green centers.

4. Coat pot with matte sealer.

5. Trim ends of wires so shamrocks are of varying lengths; glue ends of wires to ome side; glue ends of wires to one side of felt square. When dry, glue felt inside pot ¼" from top edge, sandwiching wires between felt and side of pot.

6. Fill pot with treats; personalize rim of pot with name or message, if desired, using marker. ✿

Shamrock
Cut 4 from lime green craft foam
Cut 4 from green craft foam

Let's Begin!

Materials
Both Holders

- ☐ 2 (1½"-wide) rings cut from an empty paper towel tube
- ☐ 2 (5¾" x 2") pieces green corrugated paper
- ☐ Peaks decorative paper edgers from Fiskars
- ☐ Woodsies wooden cutouts from Forster: 8 large (1½") eggs and 8 small (⅜") wings
- ☐ Premium-Coat acrylic paints from Aleene's: medium orange #OC 114, medium yellow #OC 126, medium turquoise #OC 144, medium violet #OC 162, medium fuchsia #OC 168, black #OC 176
- ☐ Scribbles 3D paints from Duncan Enterprises: white #SC 110, bright yellow #SC 112, pink surprise #SC 143
- ☐ Matte sealer
- ☐ Craft cement
- ☐ Fine-point black permanent marker
- ☐ Toothpicks
- ☐ Small paintbrush

Project Notes
Refer to photo throughout.

Let all paints, ink and sealer dry between applications.

Instructions
1. Paint four eggs and all wings medium yellow for chicks; for Easter eggs, paint one egg each medium turquoise, medium fuchsia, medium violet and medium orange.

2. *Chicks:* Using toothpick and black paint, dot eyes onto each chick. Using toothpick or tiny paint-brush, add triangular beaks and two feet to each chick with medium orange paint. Add feathers to chicks' heads with marker. Glue two wings to each chick.

3. *Easter eggs:* Decorate Easter eggs with 3D paints as desired; on sample, fuchsia and turquoise eggs are decorated with white, violet egg with pink surprise and orange egg with bright yellow.

4. Brush eggs and chicks with matte sealer.

5. Using paper edgers, trim one long edge of each piece of corrugated paper. Glue one strip around each cardboard ring.

6. Glue four eggs evenly spaced around one egg holder, and four chicks evenly spaced around the other. ✽

Easter Egg Holders

Show off the bunny's handiwork in colorful, easy cups made from green corrugated paper and wooden pieces painted in fanciful colors.

Designs by Kathy Wegner

Backside

Springtime Towel

Search your stash of fabric scraps, then create a colorful kitchen helper with your finds.

Design by June Fiechter

Let's Begin!

Materials
- □ Yellow dish towel
- □ Fabric scraps as desired (see Project Notes)
- □ HeatnBond Lite fusible webbing from Therm O Web
- □ Gold/gold #90G Metallic Knit-Cro-Sheen crochet thread from J.&P. Coats
- □ Black 6-strand embroidery floss
- □ Gold all-purpose thread
- □ ¾"-diameter flat natural wooden button
- □ Embroidery needle needle
- □ Sewing machine with zigzag stitch

Project Notes

Refer to photo and patterns throughout.

Refer to manufacturer's instructions for using fusible webbing.

On sample, blue print fabric was used for tulip; green print was used for stem and leaf; red print was used for flowerpot, with a coordinating red for band on pot; tan/gold print was used for bunny; a scrap of red print was used for ladybug; dark green solid was used for base.

Instructions

1. Launder towel and fabrics without using fabric softener; dry and press to remove wrinkles.

2. Fuse webbing to wrong side of appliqué fabrics. Transfer patterns (face down) onto paper side of fused fabric; cut out. Position appliqués on towel and fuse in place.

3. Set sewing machine for a tiny zigzag stitch just large enough to clear the width of the crochet thread; thread machine with gold all-purpose thread.

4. Lay crochet thread around each piece to outline it and zigzag over thread to hold it in place. In same fashion, add ladybug's antenna.

5. Using 6-strands black embroidery floss throughout, add ladybug's head with long stitches; add French knot eye to bunny and spot on ladybug; using gold all-purpose thread, give bunny a nose with a few short straight stitches, and sew button to bunny for tail. ❀

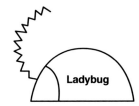

Ladybug

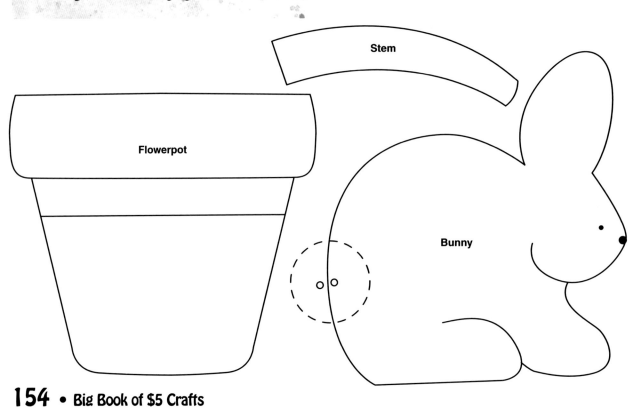

Stem

Flowerpot

Bunny

Base

Leaf

Tulip

Spring Fling Easter Critters

Created from snap-together plastic ornaments, these colorful creatures will add fun and color to your Easter buffet or springtime tea!

Designs by Veleta "Sam" Stafney

Project Notes

Refer to photo and patterns throughout.

Let all paints, ink and varnish dry between applications.

Bunny

1. Paint bead, ⅜" furniture buttons and eggcup titanium white; paint ¼" furniture button baby pink; paint heart lamp black.

2. Glue eggcup to center of heart. Coat with varnish.

3. Fill plastic ornament with Easter grass and snap halves together; trim off any grass sticking out from sides. Glue rounded end of ornament into eggcup.

4. Glue pink furniture button to center of bead for nose; glue ⅜" furniture buttons below it for muzzle.

5. Using tip of paintbrush handle dipped in lamp black, dot on black eyes. Using a stylus or toothpick, add a tiny titanium white highlight dot to each eye and a white comma stroke to nose. Lightly brush coral rose onto each cheek and muzzle. Draw eyelashes with black marking pen.

6. Coat head with varnish and glue to top of body. (Make sure lobes of heart "feet" face front.)

7. Cut two ears from white felt; fold ears together along dashed lines and apply a little glue to each to give ears dimension. Brush insides of ears with cotton-tip swab and cosmetic blusher; glue one ear to each side of head.

8. Cut two arms and one sign from white craft foam; add outlines and lettering with black marking pen. Add a little blush to arms with cotton-tip swab and cosmetic blusher. Glue arms and sign to bunny so he appears to be holding sign.

9. Cut pink ribbon in half; tie each piece in a small bow; trim ends. Glue one to center top of head and one at neckline. Glue one pink pompom atop each foot.

Chick

1. Paint bead and eggcup primary yellow; paint ¼" furniture button tangelo orange; paint heart lamp black.

2. Glue eggcup to center of heart. Coat with varnish.

3. Fill plastic ornament with Easter grass and snap halves together; trim off any grass sticking out from sides. Glue rounded end of ornament into eggcup.

4. Glue tangelo orange furniture button to center of bead for nose.

5. Using tip of paintbrush handle dipped in lamp black, dot on two black eyes and larger black mouth below nose. Using a stylus or toothpick, add a tiny titanium white highlight dot to each eye and a white comma stroke to nose. Lightly brush coral rose onto each cheek. Using marking pen, draw eyelashes, eyebrows and

Let's Begin!

Materials

Each Critter

- ☐ 5½" clear plastic teardrop-shape snap-together ornament
- ☐ 3"-wide x ¼"-thick wooden heart cutout
- ☐ 1½"-diameter wooden bead with ½" hole
- ☐ ¼" wooden furniture button
- ☐ 2⅜" wooden eggcup
- ☐ ¼" paintbrush
- ☐ Stylus or toothpick
- ☐ Satin acrylic varnish
- ☐ Fabric glue
- ☐ Black fine-point marker

Bunny

- ☐ 2 (⅜") wooden furniture buttons
- ☐ Americana acrylic paints from DecoArt: titanium white #DA1, baby pink #DA31, lamp black #DA67, coral rose #DA103
- ☐ White felt
- ☐ Pink powdered cosmetic blusher
- ☐ Cotton-tip swab
- ☐ White craft foam
- ☐ Small handful blue Easter grass
- ☐ ½ yard (⅜"-wide) light pink satin ribbon
- ☐ 2 (¾") pink pompoms

Chick

- ☐ Americana acrylic paints from DecoArt: titanium white #DA1, lamp black #DA67, coral rose #DA103, tangelo orange #DA196, primary yellow #DA201
- ☐ Yellow craft foam
- ☐ Small handful yellow Easter grass
- ☐ Light green satin ribbon: ⅓ yard each 1"-wide and ¼"-wide
- ☐ 2 (¾") yellow pompoms

mouth lines.

6. Coat head with varnish and glue to top of body. (Make sure lobes of heart "feet" face front.)

7. Cut one set of head feathers and two wings from yellow craft foam; cut feather slits as indicated. Glue wings to sides of body and head feathers to hole in top of head.

8. Tie each piece of ribbon in a bow. Glue bow of ¼" ribbon at base of head feathers. Glue bow of 1" ribbon to plastic neck about ½" below head bead. Glue one yellow pompom atop each foot. ❀

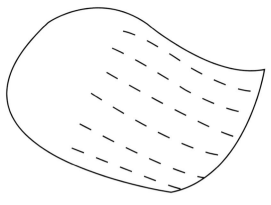

Chick Wing
Cut 2 from yellow
craft foam

Sign
Cut 1 from white craft foam

Bunny Ear
Cut 2 from white felt

Chick Head Feather
Cut 1 from yellow craft foam

Bunny Arm
Cut 2 from
white felt

Foam Curler Bunnies

Old foam curlers take on new life as cute little Easter bunnies! Let them parade down your holiday table—or hold place cards for your guests.

Designs by Veleta "Sam" Stafney

Let's Begin!

Materials
Both Bunnies

- [ ] 2 jumbo (1½" x 3⅛") pink foam curlers
- [ ] Round wooden beads: 2 (1¼") with ½" hole; 8 (⅜") with ⅛" hole
- [ ] Wooden furniture buttons: 2 (¼") and 4 (⅜")
- [ ] 4 wooden craft picks
- [ ] Americana acrylic paints from DecoArt: titanium white #DA1, baby pink #DA31, lamp black #DA67, blush flesh #DA110
- [ ] Acrylic satin varnish
- [ ] ¼" paintbrush
- [ ] Stylus or toothpick
- [ ] Torn strips of green fabric: 2" x 20" and ¾" x 20"
- [ ] Matching sewing thread and needle
- [ ] 9" x 12" pieces felt: plum and white
- [ ] Pink embroidery floss and needle
- [ ] 3" white crocheted hat
- [ ] Miniature carrots: 3 (1") and 1 (1½")
- [ ] ½" orange button
- [ ] Fine-point black permanent marker
- [ ] Cotton-tip swab
- [ ] Powdered cosmetic blusher
- [ ] Fabric glue

Project Notes

Refer to photo, patterns and Fig. 1 throughout.

Let all paints and ink dry between applications.

Each Bunny

1. Open curler; remove foam roller and set aside plastic parts for legs. Paint foam titanium white.

2. *Legs:* Using scissors and referring to Fig. 1, cut off bottom of plastic clip (the part that would snap curler closed). Paint remaining plastic parts titanium white. Apply glue to curler stem; reinsert into painted foam (body).

3. *Head:* Paint 1¼" wooden bead (head) and 2 (⅜") furniture buttons (muzzle) titanium white; paint 1/4" furniture button (nose) baby pink. Glue muzzles to lower face; glue nose centered above them. Dip stylus in black paint; dot on two eyes. Dip stylus in titanium white; add comma stroke to nose. With cotton-tip swab, lightly blush cheeks with blush flesh; dot titanium white highlight on each cheek with stylus. Using fine-point marker, draw eyelashes and add freckles to muzzles. Glue head to top of foam body. Coat with varnish.

4. *Arms, hands, legs and feet:* Paint craft picks and 4 small beads titanium white. Clip 1½" off rounded end of each pick. Apply glue to pointed ends; push into sides of foam body ¼" for arms. Glue bead to end of each arm and to end of each plastic leg.

5. *Ears:* Cut two ears from white felt. Fold each in half along dashed line; glue to hold. Color inner ears with blusher applied with swab. Glue one straight edge of ear to each side of hole in top of head, positioning Mrs. Bunny's ears so that they hang down sides of head and Mr. Bunny's so that they stand up.

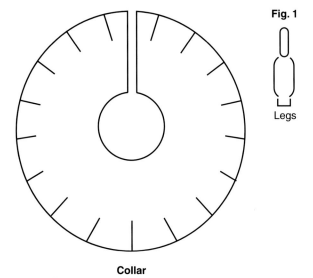

Fig. 1

Legs

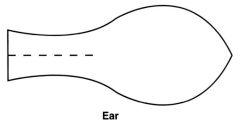

Ear
Cut 2 from white felt for each bunny

Collar
Cut 1 from plum felt for each bunny

Mrs. Bunny

1. *Dress:* Right sides facing, glue or sew short ends of 2" x 20" fabric strip together; turn right side out. With needle and thread sew gathering stitch around one edge; place skirt around curler body with opening in back; pull thread tight; knot and clip ends.

2. *Collar:* Cut collar from plum felt. Using 2 strands pink floss, sew buttonhole stitch around outer edge. Place collar around neck with opening in back; glue to hold.

3. Glue hat on top of head. Cut remaining fabric strip in half; tie each in a small bow. Glue one to crown of hat and one to collar. Glue 1" carrot in one hand.

Mr. Bunny

1. *Clothes:* Cut 2" x 4½" strip plum felt; wrap around body, overlapping ends in back. Cut off excess and glue to hold.

Add collar as in step 2 for Mrs. Bunny.

2. Glue 1" carrot to collar and another to one hand. Glue button to bunny's belly. Glue point of larger carrot between ears in hole in head. ❀

Patriotic Bead Dolls

Tiny little people made of painted wooden beads will liven up your Independence Day festivities.

Designs by Mary Ayres

Let's Begin!

Materials
Both Dolls

- ☐ Round wooden beads: 2 (1"-diameter), 2 (⅝"-diameter) and 8 (⁵⁄₁₆"-diameter)
- ☐ ⅝" wooden flowerpot
- ☐ 2 (7") pieces ¼"-wide blue satin ribbon
- ☐ 2 yards red 20-gauge wire from Artistic Wire Ltd.
- ☐ Americana acrylic paints from DecoArt: white wash #DA2, Williamsburg blue #DA40, mocha #DA60, lamp black #DA67, true red #DA129
- ☐ Paintbrushes: #6 round bristle and #6 soft round
- ☐ Black fine-tip permanent marking pen
- ☐ Tacky craft glue
- ☐ ⅛"-diameter dowel
- ☐ Wire cutters

Project Notes

Refer to photo and patterns throughout.

Refer to directions for dry-brushing and rouging under "Painting Techniques" in General Instructions on page 191.

Let all applications of paint, ink and finish dry between applications.

Girl Doll

1. Paint ⅝" bead and two ⁵⁄₁₆" beads with mocha; paint two ⁵⁄₁₆" beads lamp black.

2. Paint 1" bead true red; using end of brush handle dipped in Williamsburg blue, dot spots all over body.

3. Rouge cheeks with true red; add eyes with black marking pen.

4. Cut two 8" pieces wire for arms and two 10" pieces for legs. Thread all wire ends through head bead leaving 2½" ends extending from top for hair. Bend these ends over sides of head. Bend ends of arm wires to sides at bottom of head hole; thread leg wires through body bead. Bend ends of leg wires to sides at bottom of body bead.

5. Coil arms, legs and hair around ⅛" dowel, leaving ½" unwrapped at ends of arms and legs for attaching hands and shoes.

6. Thread mocha ⁵⁄₁₆" beads onto ends of arm wires and black beads onto ends of legs. Bend wire ends over beads toward back to hold hands and shoes in place. Shape arms, legs and hair.

7. Tie one piece of ribbon in a bow and trim ends. Glue bow to neck at center front.

Boy Doll

1. Repeat step 1 for girl doll.

2. Paint flowerpot (hat) and top half of 1" bead Williamsburg blue; dry-brush hat and blue portion of body with white wash. Paint other half of body true red.

3. Repeat step 3 for girl doll.

4. Cut two 8" pieces wire for arms and two 10" pieces for legs. Thread all wire ends through hat leaving 1½" ends extending from top. Bend these ends over sides of hat. Thread long ends of wires through head. Bend ends of arm wires to sides at bottom of head hole; thread leg wires through body bead. Bend ends of leg wires to sides at bottom of body bead.

5. Coil arms, legs and wire ends at top of hat around ⅛" dowel, leaving ½" unwrapped at ends of arms and legs for attaching hands and shoes.

6. Repeat steps 6 and 7 for girl doll. ✺

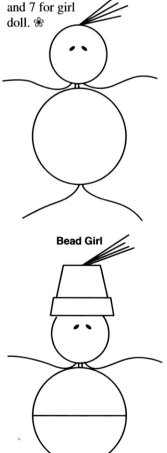

Bead Girl

Bead Boy

Stars & Heart Box

Don't save this pretty painted box only for Independence Day! It's pretty enough to leave out all year long.

Design by Paula Bales

Project Note

Refer to photo and pattern (page 165) throughout.

Instructions

1. Make separate paper patterns for two halves of heart pattern and upper left portion of heart. Dampen sponges; wrap in paper toweling and squeeze out excess water. Place each pattern on sponge and draw around it with black marker. Cut out shapes and rinse out as much of the black ink as possible.

2. Squeeze buttermilk paint onto a paper plate or other palette; dip sponge for one half of heart into paint, then blot excess onto a clean area of the plate. Place sponge on box lid and apply pressure with the palm of your hand. In same manner, sponge on other half of heart using buttermilk; let dry.

3. Using same method, sponge upper left portion of heart using uniform blue. Let dry.

4. Transfer lettering and stripes on heart to box lid.

Let's Begin!

Materials

- ☐ 6" square papier-mâché box with lid
- ☐ 1¾" Woodsies wooden star from Forster Inc.
- ☐ Americana acrylic paints from DecoArt: buttermilk #DA3, uniform blue #DA86, deep burgundy #DA128, true ochre #DA143
- ☐ #6 shader paintbrush
- ☐ Household sponges
- ☐ Tracing paper
- ☐ ZIG Millennium .05 black marker from EK Success Ltd.
- ☐ Hot-glue gun

Paint every other stripe deep burgundy. Paint wooden star true ochre. Let dry.

5. Go over lettering, outlines and stripes with black marker; add outline around edge of box lid and star shape. Glue star over blue portion of heart. ❃

Pattern on page 165

Tin-Can Luminaria

Whip up a batch of this simple, colorful candle lantern for your holiday celebration—or for any gathering where festive lighting is in order.

Design by Bev Shenefield

Let's Begin!

Materials

Luminaria

- Clean, tall spaghetti-sauce can, labels and one end removed
- Hammer and nail
- Cosmetic sponge
- Marvy fine-line Liquid Gold pen
- Rust-resistant spray primer
- Flat white spray paint
- PermEnamel paints from Delta: classic navy blue #45016, red red #45033
- PermEnamel products from Delta: surface conditioner and clear gloss glaze
- Goo Gone

Candle

- Clean 8-ounce tomato-sauce can, one end removed
- Discarded candles and/or candle ends
- Candle wicking
- Vegetable oil
- Essential oil (optional)
- Heavy saucepan and larger can to fit in it

Project Notes

Refer to photo throughout.

Let all applications of primer, sealer, paint, ink and glaze dry between applications.

Look for candles—including used and/or broken ones—at yard sales and thrift stores. They are perfect for making your own candles and are much less expensive than new candles.

Luminaria

1. Remove label glue from spaghetti sauce can with Goo Gone. Wash and rinse well; let dry. Fill can with water and freeze 24 hours or until solidly frozen.

2. Place pattern on can with seam in back; tape in place with masking tape if desired. Lay can on heavy towel. With hammer and nail, punch holes around edge of pattern, replacing can in freezer to refreeze as necessary.

3. When can is punched, let water melt and dry can thoroughly. Spray with primer, then with flat white spray paint.

4. Using sponge, paint firecrackers with red red stripes; sponge every other stripe on can with classic navy blue.

5. Add outlines of motifs and stripes and lettering with gold pen. Coat cans with clear gloss glaze.

Recycled Candle

1. Coat inside of small can with oil; pour out excess.

2. Tie wick around pencil; lay pencil across top of can and adjust till wick hangs straight to the bottom in center.

3. Place odds and ends of *Continued on page 165*

Liberty

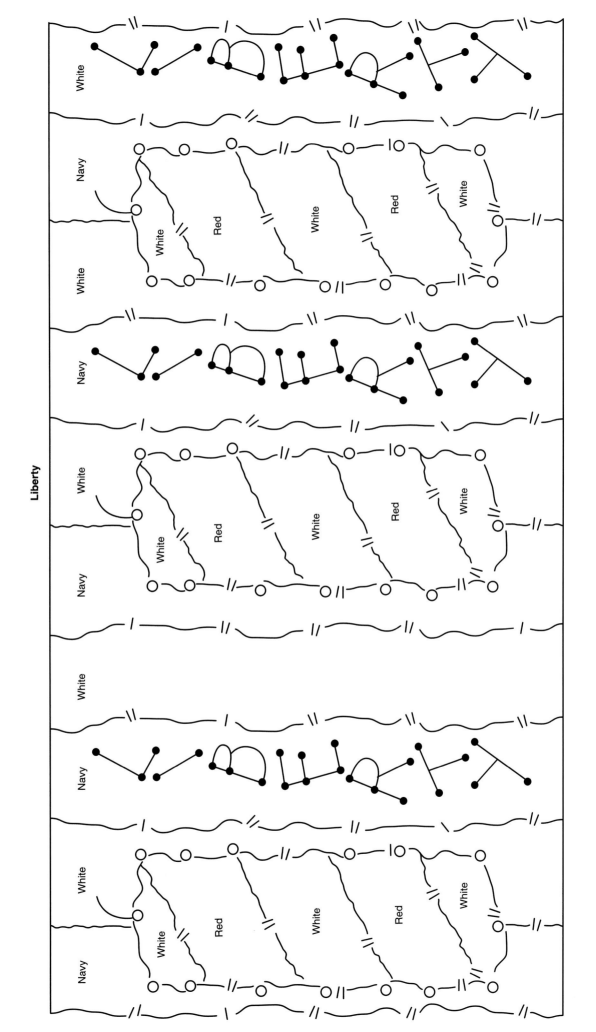

Tube Sock Witch

Add this charming miss to your Halloween decor. She's dressed in seasonal fabrics and her body is made of inexpensive socks!

Design by Veleta "Sam" Stafney

Let's Begin!

Materials

- ☐ 1 pair men's white over-the-calf tube socks, shoe size 6–13
- ☐ 1 package black fabric dye
- ☐ 6" square muslin
- ☐ ½" wooden mushroom button
- ☐ 2 packages black-and-gray two-tone Original-Curl curly hair from One & Only Creations
- ☐ Americana acrylic paints from DecoArt: titanium white #DA2, lamp black #DA67, coral rose #DA103
- ☐ ½" paintbrush
- ☐ Stylus or toothpick
- ☐ ¼ yard multicolored orange Halloween fabric
- ☐ 5" black felt witch hat
- ☐ Black fine-point permanent marking pen
- ☐ Fabric glue
- ☐ 1 cup plastic doll pellets
- ☐ Polyester fiberfill
- ☐ Sewing needle and doll needle
- ☐ Black carpet thread and sewing threads

Project Notes

Refer to photo and pattern throughout.

Follow manufacturer's instructions for using dye.

Let all paints and ink dry between applications.

Instructions

1. Dye socks with fabric dye; dry thoroughly.

2. *Body:* Cut cuff plus 2" off one sock; discard cuff piece. Turn remaining piece wrong side out. Pour pellets into sock and stuff with polyester fiberfill until semi-firm. Sew basting stitch along raw edge; pull gathers tight and knot.

3. *Head:* Thread doll needle with long length of carpet thread; knot ends. Insert needle 4½" down from gathered raw edge (step 2); wrap thread twice around sock widthwise. Pull threads tightly to indent for head; knot thread.

4. *Arms:* Cut cuff off one sock and discard cuff. From raw edge cut two 6" rings. For each arm, sew basting stitch along one raw edge. Pull gathers tight and knot. Turn wrong side out and stuff semi-firm. Sew basting stitch along other raw edge; pull gathers tight and knot.

5. *Hands:* Attach double strand of carpet thread 2" from one gathered edge of one arm. Wrap thread twice around arm; pull tight to indent for hand. Knot thread. Repeat with other arm.

6. *Connecting:* Thread doll needle with extra-long double strand of carpet thread; knot ends. Insert needle into side of body 2" below neck; run needle through body, out other side and through arm. Insert needle back through same arm, through body and through other arm. Repeat twice, pulling thread tight. Insert needle through one arm and bring it out between arm and body; pull thread tight and knot ends.

7. *Face:* Cut face pattern from muslin. Sew basting stitch along outer edge; gather slightly. Pin face to face area on sock head, adjusting gathers and smoothing wrinkles. Hand-sew around edge to secure muslin to head.

8. *Facial features:* Paint

wooden button coral rose. Glue to center of muslin face for nose. Dip end of paintbrush handle in lamp black; dot on two eyes. Apply coral rose to cheeks for blush. Using stylus, add tiny titanium white highlight dots to eyes and cheeks; add titanium white comma stroke to nose. Using black fine-point marker, add eyebrows, mouth and freckles to cheeks.

9. *Clothes:* From fabric, tear 5½"x 42" piece for skirt. With right sides facing, sew or glue 5½" edges together. Sew basting stitch along one raw edge; turn right side

out and place around body. Pull gathers tight; knot thread ends.

10. *Hair:* Loosely wrap a couple of strands of hair 10 times around four fingers. Twist hair in center and glue to top of head. Continue gluing bundles of hair, filling in sides and back of head. Fluff hair; trim loose ends.

11. Glue hat to head off to one side. Tear 2" x 45" strip Halloween fabric; cut in half to make two 2" x 22½" strips. Tie each in a bow and trim ends. Glue one bow to hat and the second to front neckline. ❀

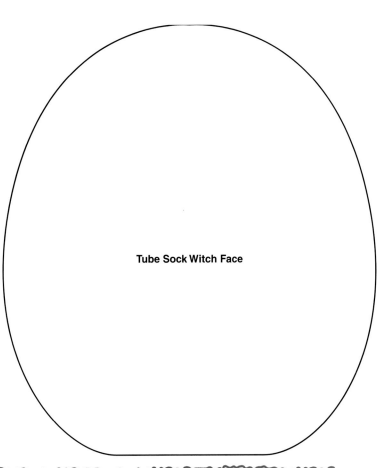

Tube Sock Witch Face

Stars & Heart Box continued from page 161

Stars and Hearts Forever!

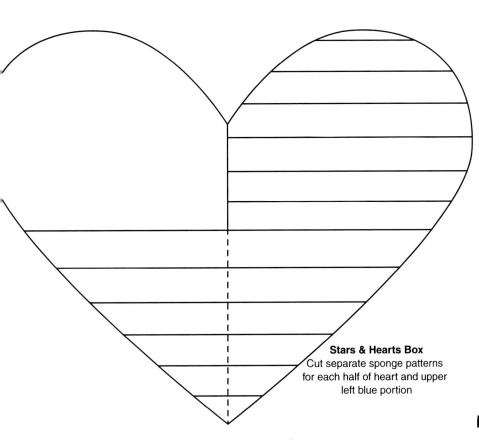

Stars & Hearts Box
Cut separate sponge patterns for each half of heart and upper left blue portion

Tin-Can Luminaria
continued from
page 162

candles in larger can; set in pan of hot water and very carefully melt candles over low heat. Add essential oil if desired.

4. Carefully pour melted wax into prepared can to within about ½" of top. Adjust wick as necessary and set aside to harden completely. If wax sinks in the center, add a little more melted wax.

5. When candle is completely hardened, carefully lift it out of the can with the pencil, taking care not to break the wick. If candle resists, run hot water over sides and bottom of can and twist it gently until it releases. Trim wick to about ½" long.

6. Insert candle in luminaria. ❀

Jack-o'-Lantern Box

Filled with treats or simply used as a decorative accent, this winsome box will bring a smile from all who see it.

Design by Chris Malone

Let's Begin!

Materials

- 5" papier-mâché pumpkin box with lid from Provo Craft
- 1" wooden ball knob
- Americana acrylic paints from DecoArt: holly green #DA48, lamp black #DA67, tangelo orange #DA196
- Spray matte finish
- 2" x 5" piece kelly green Easy Felt from CPE Inc.
- 48" piece 30-gauge green florist wire
- Paintbrushes: flat brush and liner
- Old toothbrush
- Craft glue
- Embroidery needle

Project Notes

Refer to photo and patterns throughout.

Refer to directions for base-coating under "Painting Techniques" in General Instructions on page 191.

Let all paints and finish dry between applications.

Instructions

1. Base-coat exterior surfaces of lid and box except stem area with tangelo orange. Base-coat stem area with holly green and ball knob with lamp black.

2. Paint eyes and mouth on box lid with lamp black. Using liner, add black lines at ends of smile. Glue black ball knob to center of face for nose.

3. Thin a little black paint with water. Dip toothbrush in mixture. Holding brush about 12" from box, run thumb across bristles to lightly spatter box and lid.

4. Spray painted surfaces with two coats of acrylic finish.

5. Cut three leaves from felt. Cut wire in half. Using embroidery needle, poke two small holes on each side of stem on edge of box lid and one hole in base of each leaf. Poke end of one piece of wire into hole in leaf; pull about 10" of wire through. Curl this end and several inches of wire on other side of leaf around a pencil. Insert other end of same wire into box through one hole in stem and out through second hole. Add leaf to other end of wire and curl wire in front of and behind leaf as before. Repeat on other side of stem with remaining piece of wire and remaining one leaf. Trim wire ends as desired. ✿

Halloween Puzzle Pins

Salvage lonesome puzzle pieces by giving them new life as cute and whimsical pins!

Designs by Ann Butler

Let's Begin!

Materials
Both Pins

- ☐ 2 puzzle pieces
- ☐ Acrylic paints: orange and white
- ☐ Green dimensional craft paint
- ☐ Fine-point black permanent marker
- ☐ 2 (1") pin backs
- ☐ Small paintbrush
- ☐ Craft cement or hot glue

Project Notes
Refer to photo throughout.

Let all paints and ink dry between applications

Jack-o'-Lantern
1. Paint all surfaces of puzzle piece orange.

2. Add leaves with green dimensional paint.

3. Using marking pen, draw jack-o'-lantern face; blacken stem; outline leaves and add veins on top of them; draw dashed outline around puzzle piece.

4. Glue pin back onto wrong side of pin.

Ghost
1. Paint all surfaces of puzzle piece white.

2. Using marking pen, draw face and dashed outline around puzzle piece.

3. Glue pin back onto wrong side of pin. ✿

Jack-o'-Lantern Box

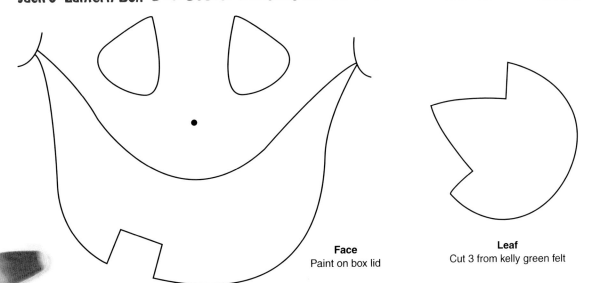

Face
Paint on box lid

Leaf
Cut 3 from kelly green felt

Pumpkin Candle Holders

Easy and inexpensive, these candle holders bring a dash of vibrant autumn color to your table.

Design by Veleta "Sam" Stafney

Let's Begin!

Materials

Two Candle Holders

- ☐ Wooden products: 4 (1½" x 2⅛") spools, 2 (1½") candle cups, 2 (3"-wide, ¼"-thick) hearts, 2 (¼") furniture buttons, 2 (2" x ⅞") ovals, 2 craft sticks
- ☐ Americana acrylic paints from DecoArt: titanium white #DA1, lamp black #DA67, Hauser dark green #DA133, tangelo orange #DA196
- ☐ ¼" paintbrush
- ☐ Stylus or toothpick
- ☐ Cotton-tip swab
- ☐ Acrylic satin varnish
- ☐ ¼ yard fall print fabric
- ☐ 6" square pirate green felt
- ☐ 2 (2½"-diameter) straw scarecrow hats from Darice
- ☐ Fabric glue
- ☐ 4 (⅜") flat orange buttons
- ☐ 2 (8") hunter green tapers
- ☐ Black fine-point permanent marking pen
- ☐ Polyester fiberfill
- ☐ Coordinating sewing threads and hand-sewing needle

Project Notes

Refer to photo and pattern throughout.

Let all coats of paint, ink and varnish dry between applications.

Following instructions are for one candle holder; repeat to make second.

Painting & Assembly

1. Paint wooden pieces as follows, adding an additional coat as needed: *tangelo orange*—two spools, candle cup, oval and craft pick; *Hauser dark green*—heart; *lamp black*—furniture button.

2. *Body:* Glue two spools together end to end for body; let dry. Glue candle cup to top of spools; glue heart to other end. (Lobes of heart will be front of candle holder.)

3. *Face:* Glue furniture button to center of candle cup. Using tip of paintbrush handle dipped in lamp black, dot on two eyes. Using black pen, add eyelashes, eyebrows and mouth. Using stylus dipped in titanium white, add tiny highlight dot to each eye and comma stroke to nose. Apply titanium white lightly to cheeks for blush.

4. Apply varnish to entire body, head and heart base.

Clothing

1. Tear all pieces of fabric: 3" x 22" for dress, 3" x 10" for arms, two 1" x 22" strips for bows, and ¾" square for patch on hat.

2. *Dress:* Right sides facing, glue together 3" ends of 3" x 22" piece. Sew basting stitch along one raw edge. Turn fabric right side out. Place dress around body and pull gathers tight around neck of candle cup; knot thread and clip ends.

3. *Arms:* With right sides out, fold 3" x 10" piece in thirds lengthwise. Glue raw edges down leaving ends open. Sew basting stitch across center of arm piece; pull thread tight and knot. Stuff each arm lightly. Overlap short edges ¼" and sew a basting stitch through all layers; pull thread tight, knot and clip ends. Place arms over dress with raw edges in back; glue at back of neck.

4. *Collar:* Cut from pirate green felt; cut 1¼" circle from center and cut through one side. Place collar around neck with opening in back. Glue collar in place.

Finishing

1. *Hat:* Cut out center of crown of straw hat. Slip hat down over tapered end of candle; seat candle in candle-cup head. Push hat

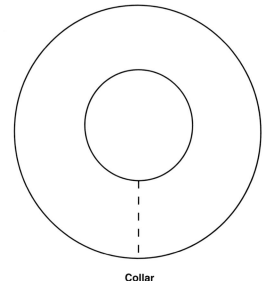

Collar
Cut 1 from pirate green felt

down until it sits on top of head. Glue fabric patch off to one side on hat; glue button in center of patch.

2. *Bows:* Tie each 1" x 22" fabric strip in a bow. Glue one to neck of dress at center front, and one to heart base, off to one side. Glue button to center of bow on heart base.

3. *Sign:* Glue craft pick to back of painted wooden oval; draw stitching lines around oval with black marking pen and write "HAPPY" in center. ***Note:*** *On second oval, write "HALLOWEEN."* Varnish sign; spot-glue to arm. ❁

Thanksgiving Place Cards

Check out the scrapbooking sections of craft stores for a variety of colored card stock available by the sheet.

Designs by Chris Malone

Project Note

Refer to photo and patterns throughout.

Pumpkin

1. Fold 3½" x 5" card stock in half to measure 3½" x 2½".

2. Cut pumpkin from orange card stock; cut stem and leaf from green corrugated paper.

3. Poke small hole in wide end of leaf and insert end of wire, leaving 2" of wire behind leaf. Curl both wire ends around a pencil, leaving center 1" of wire straight. Glue wire tendrils to top center of place card. Bend wire around base of stem; glue stem to place card; glue pumpkin over stem and wire.

4. Emboss name on cream card stock or write with black marker; glue to center of pumpkin.

Leaves & Acorns

1. Fold 3½" x 5" card stock in half to measure 3½" x 2½".

2. Cut one leaf from gold card stock and another from rust; cut freehand "veins" from dark brown and glue one down center of each leaf.

3. Glue textured brown paper to card stock. Glue leaves in upper right corner.

4. Emboss name on orange card stock or write with black marker; glue to center of brown paper.

5. Using 2 or 3 strands raffia, tie a simple 2¾"–3" overhand bow; trim ends and glue to bottom left corner of place card. Glue acorns over bow.

Let's Begin!

Materials

Each Place Card

- Black medium marking pen *or* alphabet rubber stamp set with black embossing powder and heat tool
- Craft glue

Pumpkin

- Card stock: 3½" x 5" piece buff, 3¼" x 2" orange and 1" x 1⅞" piece cream
- Scrap of green corrugated paper
- 12" piece 22-gauge green florist wire

Leaves & Acorns

- Card stock: 3½" x 5" piece cream, 1" x 1⅞" piece orange, 2½" x 1¾" piece each gold and rust, and scraps of dark brown
- 3" x 2" piece textured brown paper cut from hot-cup sleeve
- 2 small acorns
- A few strands of natural raffia

Turkey

- Card stock: 3½" x 5" piece buff, 1" x 1⅞" piece orange, small pieces of dark rust, gold, burgundy, dark brown and orange
- 3" x 2" piece off-white corrugated paper cut from light-bulb packaging
- 2 (4mm) black half-beads

Turkey Place Card
Cut turkey head and body from dark rust card stock;
cut wing and beak from gold;
cut wattle from burgundy;
cut feet from brown;
cut feathers from assorted colors

Pumpkin Place Card
Cut 1 pumpkin from orange card stock;
cut stem and leaf from green corrugated paper

Painted Pumpkin Doily
Instructions begin on page 172

Turkey

1. Fold 3½" x 5" card stock in half to measure 3½" x 2½".

2. Glue corrugated off-white paper to card stock. Emboss name on orange card stock or write with black marker; glue to corrugated paper so left edge is ¼" from edge of corrugated paper.

3. Cut head and body from dark rust card stock, wing and beak from gold, wattle from burgundy, feet from dark brown and feathers from orange, gold and burgundy. Glue turkey pieces to right side of place card as shown; glue on black half-beads for eyes. ❀

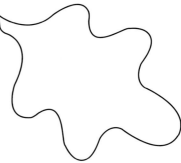

Leaves & Acorns Place Card
Cut 1 from gold
and 1 from rust card stock

Painted Pumpkin Doily

A few simple strokes of the brush yield a delightful seasonal accent. Your "canvas" is a delicate ready-made doily!

Design by Phyllis Sandford

Let's Begin!

Materials

- ☐ 9" x 5¾" white oval Battenburg doily from Wimpole Street Creations
- ☐ Starlite Shimmering Fabric Color paints from Delta: deep clover #10421, egg yolk #10433, leaf green #10439
- ☐ Fabric Dye Brush-On fabric colors from Delta: orange #10303, light brown #10315, dark brown #10316 and black #10318
- ☐ Paintbrushes: #6 and #8 shaders and #0 liner
- ☐ Stylus
- ☐ Blue graphite paper
- ☐ Tracing paper

Project Note

Refer to photo throughout.

See directions for base-coating, side-loading and highlighting in "Painting Techniques" in General Instructions on page 191.

Instructions

1. Wash and dry doily without using fabric softener; iron to remove all creases and wrinkles.

2. Trace pattern onto tracing paper; transfer to center of doily using stylus and blue graphite paper.

3. Using #8 shader, basecoat pumpkins with orange, leaves with leaf green and pumpkin stems with light brown.

4. Side-loading #6 shader, shade pumpkins with light brown, leaves with a half-and-half mixture of black and dark brown, and pumpkin stems with dark brown.

5. Highlight pumpkins with egg yolk.

6. Mix a little black with a little deep clover; add water as needed to make mixture an inky consistency. Using #0 liner, paint pumpkin vines with mixture. ❀

Photo on page 171

PAINTING KEY
X Highlighting
O Shading

COLOR KEY
Starlite Shimmering Fabric Color
DC Deep clover #10421
EY Egg yolk #10433
LG Leaf green #10439
Fabric Dye Brush-On Fabric Color
O Orange #10303
LB Light brown #10315
DB Dark brown #10316
B Black #10318
Color numbers refer to products from Delta Technical Coatings.

Painted Pumpkin Doily

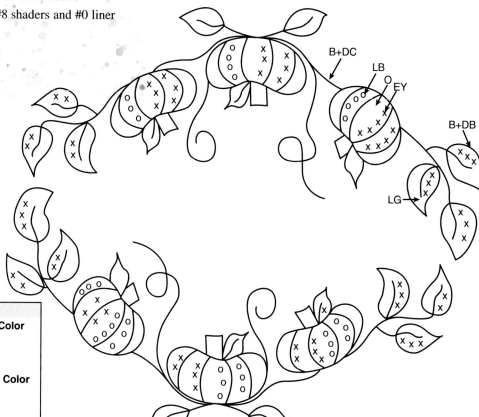

Materials

- 2¾"-diameter wooden ball-ornament cutout from Lara's Crafts
- Woodsies wooden cutouts from Forster Inc.: 7 large teardrops, 2 medium teardrops, 1 small teardrop, 1 large circle and 2 small stars
- Flat-sided napkin basket, 7" x 5¼" 3¾"
- Americana acrylic paints from DecoArt: antique gold #DA9, country red #DA18, antique white #DA58, lamp black #DA67, honey brown #DA163, milk chocolate #DA174, marigold #DA194, tangelo orange #DA196
- Paintbrushes: flat and small round
- Old toothbrush or spatter brush
- 4–6 strands natural raffia
- ⅞" flat button in coordinating color
- Black fine-line permanent marking pen
- Spray matte finish
- Permanent fabric adhesive

Project Notes

Refer to photo and pattern throughout.

Use flat brush unless noted otherwise.

Refer to directions for base-coating under "Painting Techniques" in General Instructions on page 191.

Let all applications of paint, ink and finish dry between applications.

Instructions

1. Base-coat all surfaces of wooden pieces: *antique white*—both circles; *tangelo orange*—one large and two medium teardrops; *honey brown*—two large teardrops; *marigold*—two large teardrops; *antique gold*—small teardrop and stars.

Turkey Face

Turkey Napkin Holder

Garage sales are a great source for baskets of all shapes and sizes—perfect for decorating!

Design by Chris Malone

2. Using round brush, paint country red wattle on small circle (face). Dot on eyes with tip of paintbrush handle dipped in lamp black paint.

3. Thin a little antique white paint with water. Load toothbrush with thinned mixture. Hold over large teardrops (tail feathers) and medium teardrops (wings); run thumb across bristles to spatter feathers with paint.

4. Using black pen, outline painted wattle and each painted wooden piece with a pattern of wiggly lines and dots. Add small straight eyebrows.

5. Glue head to top front of body. Glue milk chocolate tail feather to back of body at center top; glue remaining feathers down sides of body. Glue beak to face over wattle; glue wings to body. Glue stars to back of body at bottom for feet.

6. Spray assembled turkey with two coats matte finish.

7. Glue turkey to front of basket. Push raffia through open space in top right corner of basket; tie in a bow and trim ends. (Or, if basket is tightly woven, tie raffia in a bow and glue it to basket.) Glue button over center of bow. ❀

Tin-Punch Hanukkah Ornament

For the Festival of Lights, make this delightful ornament to embellish a gift, hang in a window, or suspend from a drawer pull.

Design by Sandra Graham Smith

Let's Begin!

Materials

- ☐ Wide-mouth gold canning jar lid with blank, flat top
- ☐ Glossy enamel paints: white, yellow and light blue
- ☐ Small artist paintbrush
- ☐ Black fine-line permanent marker
- ☐ 4" white paper lace doily
- ☐ Blue felt
- ☐ Black 6-strand embroidery floss and large-eye needle
- ☐ Tacky craft glue
- ☐ Pinking shears
- ☐ Pressed-wood board or other hard, protective surface
- ☐ Hammer
- ☐ Several finishing nails
- ☐ Tracing paper
- ☐ Masking tape

Project Notes

Refer to photo and pattern (page 179) throughout.

Let paints and ink dry between applications.

Painted Ornament

1. Trace pattern for menorah onto tracing paper. Cut out. Tape pattern on right side of lid.

2. Place lid on protective surface. Use hammer to tap nail from dot to dot, piercing tin. Change nail when point dulls.

3. Hold up punched lid to light; repunch any holes where necessary. Remove pattern and tape. Smooth side will be front.

4. Paint designs inside punched lines using thick strokes: *light blue*—candles; *yellow*—candelabrum and flames; *white*—disk on stem of candelabrum.

5. Using black marker draw Star of David on white disk.

Finishing

1. Using pinking shears, cut circle from blue felt.

2. Glue paper doily to center of felt; glue punched, painted ornament to center of doily.

3. Thread hanging loop of black embroidery floss through felt and doily at center top of ornament. ✿

Pattern on page 179

Christmas Gift Trio

Give those mountains of holiday cards another life as dazzling greeting cards, gift tags and gift boxes the family will love!

Designs by Judy Atwell

Project Notes

Refer to photo throughout.

General Instructions below refer to all projects; see notes for individual projects that follow.

Using the self-adhesive paper takes a little practice. If decorations shift a little when you position the self-adhesive paper, that is acceptable; don't try to be too exact.

General Instructions

1. Prepare and assemble supplies before beginning: Cut out several "centerpiece" motifs, such as the teddy bears used on sample projects. Cut scraps of Mylar and cellophane into small, manageable pieces.

Cut tinsel into short lengths. Have a piece of paper ready to receive extra glitter.

2. Measure surface to be decorated—the top of box lid, or area to be decorated on a larger lid; the cover of greeting card, envelope or gift tag. Draw identical shape on paper side of self-adhesive paper; cut out and set aside.

3. Add layers of decoration to surface to be decorated, beginning with shiny Mylar pieces and snippets of colored cellophane. Use a glue stick as needed to hold pieces in place.

4. Glue centerpiece motif in place over Mylar and

Continued on page 181

Let's Begin!

Materials
All Projects

- ☐ Clear plastic-coated self-adhesive paper
- ☐ Christmasy cutouts from greeting cards or wrapping paper
- ☐ Scraps of clear Mylar gift wrap
- ☐ Scraps of red or green cellophane
- ☐ Scraps of gold tinsel
- ☐ Glitter in desired color and/or size
- ☐ Glue stick (optional)
- ☐ Hole punch

Greeting Card

- ☐ 8½" x 11" piece white card stock (greeting card)
- ☐ 8¾" x 6" red envelope

Gift Card

- ☐ 4" x 6" blank white index card
- ☐ 10" piece gold metallic cord

Gift Box

- ☐ White gift box
- ☐ Flat-back acrylic jewels or cabochons (optional)

Pop Bottle Snowman

Perched on a counter, guarding your hearth or standing sentinel in a doorway, this frosty fellow is sure to bring warm smiles!

Design by Paula Bales

Let's Begin!

Materials

- Clean, dry 2-liter plastic soft-drink bottle with lid, label removed
- Clean, dry sand
- Plastic foam balls: 4" and 2 (1½")
- 3 long white tube socks
- Americana acrylic paints from DecoArt: Georgia clay #DA17, lamp black #DA67, Santa red #DA170
- Silver #DA70 Dazzling Metallics acrylic paint from DecoArt
- Coal black No-Prep metal paint from DecoArt
- Snow-Tex snow paste from DecoArt
- Small paintbrushes
- Empty, clean can, 3¼" tall and 3¼" in diameter
- Low-temp and hot-glue guns
- Black fine-point permanent marker
- 2 (4½") pieces 20-gauge wire
- Black felt
- 1¼" piece cut from sharpened end of sharpened pencil or dowel
- Green excelsior
- 1½" artificial bird nest
- Small artificial red bird
- Black buttons: 2 (⅜") and 4 (¾")
- Wooden spoon
- Tapestry needle
- White crochet thread
- Flannel fabric: 2½" x 30" strip and 1" x 24" strip

Project Notes

Refer to photo and pattern throughout.

Let all paints and ink dry between applications.

Instructions

1. Fill bottle half-full with sand; replace lid.

2. Push large foam ball on top of lid. Remove ball; squeeze low-temperature glue into hole and replace ball on lid. Hold firmly for a minute or two until, glue has set.

3. Slide bottle headfirst into one sock. Push to end of sock and glue edges around bottom of bottle.

4. *Arms:* Cut cuffs off two socks, cutting pieces about 7" long. Turn inside out. With needle and crochet thread, sew running stitch close to one end. Pull stitches to gather; knot. Turn right side out. Repeat with other arm piece.

5. Push small foam ball into gathered end of each sock arm. Wrap crochet thread around sock just above ball to create wrist. Knot thread; trim off excess.

6. Poke a piece of wire through center of each arm and into each foam ball. Gather remaining end of arm around wire with crochet thread. Glue close to neck.

7. Tie 2½" x 30" strip of fabric around neck for scarf; knot loosely and fray ends.

8. Dip paintbrush bristles lightly in Santa red paint; dab off excess onto paper towels. Rub brush in cir-cular motion on face for cheeks. Glue ⅜" buttons in place for eyes.

9. Paint sharpened pencil point with Georgia clay. Poke hole for nose through sock into foam ball; glue nose into hole.

10. Draw eyebrows, eyelashes and mouth with marker.

11. Glue four ¾" buttons down front of snowman's body.

12. *Shovel:* Paint bowl of wooden spoon silver; paint remainder of spoon lamp black. When dry, thickly apply snow paste to end of spoon. Glue shovel to hand and body.

13. *Hat:* Paint can with black metal paint; apply snow paste thickly to top and one side. Cut hat brim from black felt; slide brim over can and glue in place. Glue remaining fabric strip around can for hatband. Glue excelsior, bird nest and bird to hat brim; dab snow paste onto brim. Glue hat to snowman's head. ❁

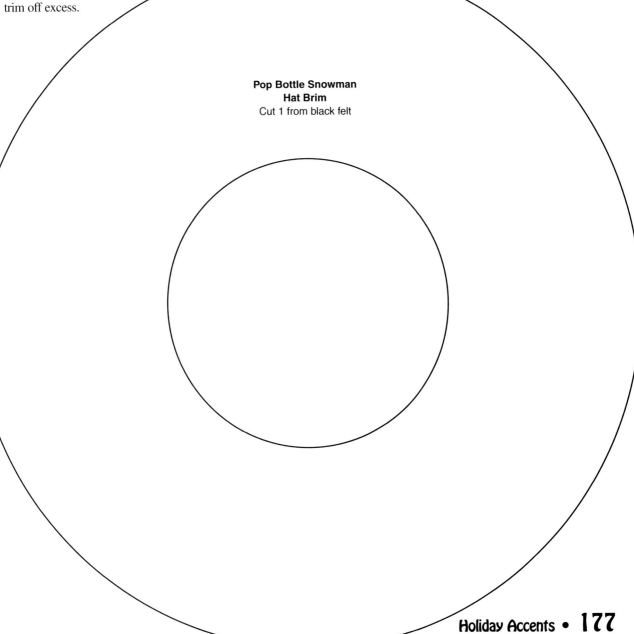

**Pop Bottle Snowman
Hat Brim
Cut 1 from black felt**

Painted Santa Cookie Tin

Stencils make it easy to achieve professional-looking results on this festive holiday cookie tin for Christmas treats!

Design by Shelia Sommers

Let's Begin!

Materials

- Plain white 7"-diameter tin with lid
- Ceramcoat acrylic paints from Delta: spice brown #2049, Quaker grey #2057, Christmas green #2068, crimson #2076, medium flesh #2126, light ivory #2401, putty #2460, Santa's flesh #2472, white #2505, black #2506, opaque yellow #2509, pink parfait #2525, chocolate cherry #2538
- 14K gold #02-604 Ceramcoat Gleams acrylic paint from Delta
- Paintbrushes: ¼" angular, #5 pouncing brush, ¼" filbert comb, 10/0 liner
- Stencil Magic precut stencils from Delta: Santa's Visit and Bah Humbug
- All-purpose metal primer from Delta
- Spray gloss varnish
- Vinegar
- Masking tape

Project Notes

Refer to photo throughout.

Stencils can be used on any type of paintable surface; they are simple to use and lend a sophisticated look to the finished project. The techniques used require more patience than artistic skills. The only rule of thumb when sponge-painting a stencil is to use very little paint. Too much paint applied at once can cause a ridge to form around the edges of the stencil, or can travel under the edges of the stencil cutout.

Refer to directions for shading in "Painting Techniques" in General

Instructions on page 191.

Preparation

1. Combine equal parts vinegar and water and thoroughly clean tin with mixture; rinse completely to remove all residues and dry with a clean, lint-free towel.

2. Apply a coat of metal primer to lid and sides of tin; let pieces dry for 24 hours to give primer time to cure and attach to the surface.

3. Add an equal amount of metal primer to each color of paint; this will help paint adhere to slick surface.

4. Secure Santa stencil on lid with masking tape. Using a piece of paper to protect areas adjacent to where you are working, paint design.

Painting

1. *Face:* Sponge with Santa flesh. Shade side next to beard with medium flesh. Thin pink parfait with enough primer to produce a transparent shade; add a cheek with mixture. Using tip of pencil or brush handle, add black eye dot; when dry, add tiny white highlight dot.

2. *Jacket and pants:* Sponge with crimson; shade with black using angular brush.

3. *Fur:* Sponge with putty. Using pouncing brush, add coat of light ivory. When dry, add a coat of white, applying color to permit each of previous coats to show through. When dry, shade with spice brown.

4. *Belt, shoes and bag:* Sponge with black; highlight bag and shoes with white.

5. *Mittens and candle:* Sponge with Christmas green. Sponge flames and glow of candle with opaque yellow. Add sufficient primer to opaque yellow to produce a transparent shade of color and add a hint of color around flame.

6. *Candle base:* Sponge with 14K gold. Using liner, add three thin crimson lines to base of candle flame.

7. *Beard:* Sponge with Quaker grey. Thin light ivory and white with primer; using comb brush, add several thin lines of light ivory followed by white, allowing each of previous colors to show through.

8. *Wording:* Place stencil of wording around sides of tin. Depending on size of tin, you may need to adjust the words to fit around the tin. Sponge letters with black, holly leaves with Christmas green, and add crimson dots with brush handle to represent berries.

9. Allow paints to dry thoroughly. Apply several coats of varnish to outside of lid and tin. ❀

Backside

Tin-Punch Hanukkah Ornament
continued from page 174

Tin-Punch Hanukkah Ornament

Darling Angel Garland

These little angels are simple to make, but they're loaded with personality! String them from tree or mantel to give your holiday decor a heavenly touch.

Design by Lee Lindeman

Let's Begin!

Materials

- ☐ 30" x 3½" strip thin wood stock
- ☐ Americana acrylic paints from DecoArt: white wash #DA2, lamp black #DA67, peony pink #DA215, soft peach #DA216
- ☐ #4 filbert paintbrush
- ☐ Fine sandpaper
- ☐ Mini jute hair
- ☐ 2 yards iridescent glitter cord
- ☐ Metallic gold cord
- ☐ Tacky craft glue and/or hot-glue gun
- ☐ Coping saw or scroll saw

Project Notes

Refer to photo and pattern throughout.

Paint all surfaces of angels. Let all paints dry between applications.

Instructions

1. Cut desired number of angels from wood (sample garland has six). Sand edges.

2. Paint angels' gowns white wash; paint heads, hands and feet soft peach.

3. Dot two black eyes on each angel's face; give each angel two round peony pink cheeks.

4. Cut mini jute hair in short lengths; glue to each angel's head.

5. Glue necklace of gold cord around each angel's neckline; glue lengths of iridescent glitter cord around each angel's head for halo and around hem of gown.

6. Thread angels onto long piece of gold cord through a loop of their hair. Space along garland as desired and secure their positions with glue as needed. ❀

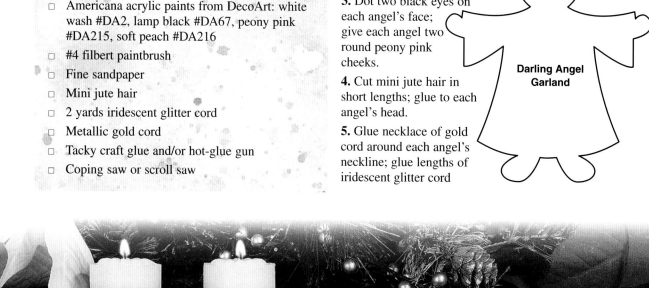

Darling Angel Garland

Recycled Gift Tags

Give old greeting cards new life as personalized gift tags for your holiday presents.

Design by Ann Butler

Let's Begin!

Materials
- ☐ Watercolor paper
- ☐ Greeting cards
- ☐ Decorative paper edgers
- ☐ Fiskars paper crimper
- ☐ Satin thread or other decorative thread or fine cord
- ☐ Round hole punch
- ☐ Craft glue

Project Note
Refer to photo throughout.

Instructions
1. Cut desired motifs from greeting cards using paper edgers; run through crimper.

2. Cut or tear watercolor paper into rectangles approximately 3" x 5" or appropriate size for your motifs. Fold each piece of watercolor paper in half. Punch hole through both layers of upper left corner.

3. Glue crimped design to front. Tie tag to gift with hanging loop of cord attached through hole. ❀

Christmas Gift Trio continued from page 175

cellophane. Arrange strands of tinsel around it; some overlap is acceptable. Sprinkle areas with glitter.

5. Remove self-adhesive paper from its backing; visually line it up with your project. Starting at bottom, firmly and slowly press contact paper upward over decorations. Use the heel of your hand and rub over the entire piece to achieve a good seal.

6. Trim any pieces of tinsel, Mylar, etc., protruding from edges.

Greeting Card
Fold 8½" x 11" piece card stock in half. Make sure centerpiece motif is in scale with card.

Gift Tag
Fold index card in half; punch hole in upper left corner. When finished decorating and applying self-adhesive paper, repunch through paper. Attach hanging loop of gold metallic cord through hole.

Gift Box
Glue on a flat-back jewel or cabochon for an extra touch.

For larger boxes, decorate a corner, the center areas, or a strip down one side of box. ❀

Evergreen & Cranberry Ornaments

Whip up a basketful of these ornaments in a single evening— then use them to deck the halls, the tree, your packages and just about anything else you can think of to add holiday cheer!

Designs by Celia Lange Designs

Let's Begin!

Materials

Both Ornaments

- ☐ 2 (12") stems of artificial mini evergreen
- ☐ 13 (¾") red wooden beads with large holes
- ☐ Decorative buttons: snowman and gingerbread man
- ☐ 12" piece (1"-wide) red-and-white gingham ribbon
- ☐ 2 (4") pieces green florist paddle wire
- ☐ Hot-glue gun

Project Note

Refer to photo throughout.

Instructions

1. Trim ribbon to make two 12" pieces each ⅓" wide, leaving one edged with red and one with white.

2. Thread six beads onto evergreen stem for round ornament and seven beads onto stem for heart-shaped ornament. Wrap ends of stems together to form two evergreen circles, then slide beads to space them evenly. Shape stem with seven beads into a heart.

3. Tie both pieces of ribbon into bows; notch ends. With paddle wire, secure bows to wreaths, forming wire hanging loops on wrong side of ornaments as you do so.

4. Snap backs off decorative buttons; glue one to center of each bow. ❀

Santa & Snowman Spoons

Here's a whimsical way to share Christmas cheer. If you don't have an odd serving spoon or two lying around, pick them up inexpensively at thrift shops or garage sales.

Designs by Barbara Matthiessen

Let's Begin!

Materials
Both Spoons

- 2 serving spoons
- No-Prep metal paints from DecoArt: bright white, coal black, real red, cornflower blue, bright orange, peach blush
- Paintbrushes: soft-bristle shader, liner and stencil brush
- Toothpick
- 1¾" x 8" torn fabric strips: red plaid and pastel plaid
- Pompoms: ⅝" pink and 1" white
- Fabric glue
- Black marking pen

Project Notes
Paint designs on convex surfaces (back sides) of spoons.

Refer to photo and patterns throughout. Adjust sizes of patterns as needed to fit your spoons.

Let all paints and ink dry between applications.

Santa
1. Wash and dry spoon. Using soft-bristled brush, paint convex surface of spoon white.

2. Paint Santa's hat red; paint face peach blush; paint nose and mouth red. Paint eyes black; dot on white highlights with toothpick.

3. Add details with black marking pen: mustache, fur hat brim and outline.

4. Cut fringe in short ends of red plaid fabric strip; tie around spoon for scarf and secure with dots of glue. Glue white pompom to tip of hat.

Snowman
1. Wash and dry spoon. Using soft-bristled brush, paint convex surface of spoon white.

2. Paint snowman's hat blue. Mix red and white paints to make pink; apply mixture to cheeks with stencil brush. Paint nose orange. Paint eyes black. Dot white highlights onto eyes (one dot) and cheeks (three dots) with toothpick.

3. Add mouth and hat brim with black marking pen.

4. Cut fringe in short ends of pastel plaid fabric strip; tie around spoon for scarf and secure with dots of glue. Glue pink pompom to tip of hat. ❀

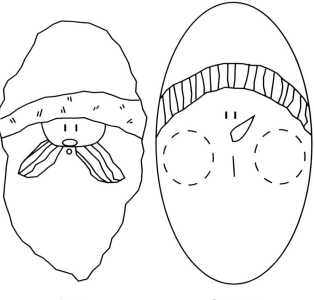

Santa   Snowman

Winter Holidays Luminarias

Use stencils and simple painting techniques to make these stunning pierced candle lanterns!

Designs by Shelia Sommers

Project Notes

Refer to photo throughout.

Stencils can be used on any type of paintable surface; they are simple to use and lend a sophisticated look to the finished project.

The techniques used require more patience than artistic skills. The only rule of thumb when sponge-painting a stencil is to use very little paint. Too much paint applied at once can cause a ridge to form around the edges of the stencil, or can travel under the edges of the stencil cutout.

Refer to directions for shading in "Painting Techniques" in General Instructions on page 191.

Let all paints and other products dry between applications.

Painting instructions are the same for both cans. However, when stenciling larger can, stencil the snow at the bottom, then adjust the design slightly upward and off-center before stenciling houses. Fill in any holes in design with trees.

Painting

1. Apply a coat of surface conditioner to exterior of cans. Follow with two or three coats of metal primer. Dry completely.

2. Base-coat exterior of cans with sufficient coats of midnight paint to produce an opaque shade.

3. Wrap stencil around can, attaching it with masking tape at top or bottom where there is no paint.

4. *Barn roof and church:* Sponge softly with ultra white allowing a hint of the base coat to show through.

5. *Tree:* Sponge foliage true green and trunks with chocolate brown. Shade back of each branch with mallard green. Softly sponge ultra white onto tips of foliage.

6. *Barn:* Sponge with country tomato; sponge weathervane with dark goldenrod. Shade under roofline with midnight.

7. *Church:* Sponge sides with slate, doors and cross on top of steeple with chocolate brown, and bell with dark goldenrod.

8. *House:* Sponge sides khaki and make roof and door chocolate brown; sponge chimney khaki and smoke mushroom; shade bottom of chimney with midnight. Shade each puff of smoke and under roofline onto house with chocolate brown. Highlight smoke and dab white onto roofline.

9. *Snow and snowflakes:* Stencil and dot with ultra white. Thin a little ultra white with clear gloss glaze to produce a transparent shade and add a wash under each pile of snow and in front of the doors on each building.

10. Using liner, dab snow on very tips of tree branches, tops of each roof, weathervanes and crosses on top of churches. Add windowpanes to churches and houses, dabbing snow at tops of doors. Outline barn door, adding an "X" across center.

11. When paint is dry, coat painted surfaces with clear gloss glaze.

12. Fill cans with water; place in freezer overnight. Once water is frozen completely, use hammer and nails to punch holes in center of each larger snowflake. Add smaller holes to sky using smaller nail to represent stars. Let water melt; empty and dry.

13. Place candles in finished luminarias. ❈

Let's Begin!

Materials

- ☐ 1-gallon and 1-quart paint cans, washed, dried and labels removed
- ☐ PermEnamel paints from Delta: chocolate #45004, true green #45012, country tomato #45017, mushroom #45018, light khaki #45021, ultra white #45029, mallard green #45031, midnight #45116, slate #45124, pine green #45129
- ☐ PermEnamel products from Delta: metal primer, surface conditioner and clear gloss glaze
- ☐ Paintbrushes: ¼" angular, 1" and #1 flats
- ☐ Snowy Magic Stencil Magic precut stencil from Delta
- ☐ Vinegar
- ☐ Masking tape

Ginger Stars Gift Bag

Give extra punch to those gifts of home-baked goodies when you present them in this cute—and simple!—paper tote.

Design by Kathy Wegner

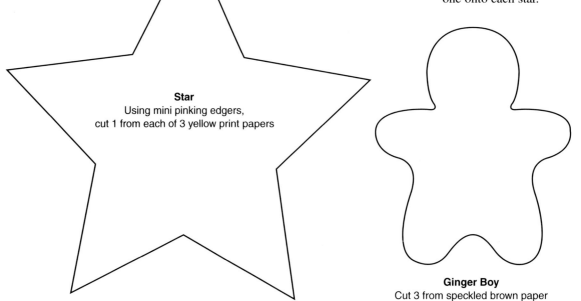

Let's Begin!

Materials
- 9¾" x 7¾" kraft paper bag with handles
- Decorative scrapbook papers: 4½" square in each of three yellow prints; 3" x 7" piece speckled brown
- 4½" square kraft paper
- PeelnStick double-sided adhesive sheet from Therm O Web
- Mini-Pinking decorative paper edgers from Fiskars
- Black fine-point permanent marker
- 12" piece natural jute
- ¼" round hole punch

Project Notes
Refer to photo and patterns throughout.

Refer to manufacturer's instructions for using adhesive sheet.

Instructions
1. Apply pieces of adhesive sheet to backs of yellow and speckled brown papers.

2. Using mini-pinking paper edgers, cut star from each piece of yellow paper; using regular scissors, cut three ginger boys from brown speckled paper.

3. Peel backing from stars; press two onto front of bag; press third onto kraft paper square. Peel backing from ginger boys; press one onto each star.

Star
Using mini pinking edgers,
cut 1 from each of 3 yellow print papers

Ginger Boy
Cut 3 from speckled brown paper

4. Using mini-pinking edgers, trim excess kraft paper from around star on kraft paper square.

5. Using marker, add "running stitch" outline around stars and ginger boys; dot eyes and add smiles to ginger boys; draw a broken line connecting stars on gift bag.

6. Punch two holes about ½" apart—like buttonholes—through center of separate ginger star. Tie this star to bag handle with jute, passing ends of jute through holes and tying them in a bow on front. ❧

Winter Friends Wall Plaque

You can make this charming accent in a snap with the help of preprinted paper.

Design by Tina Wheeler

Let's Begin!

Materials

- ☐ 1 sheet Winter Friends paper from Provo Craft
- ☐ No-wrinkle rubber cement
- ☐ Paintbrushes: flat and liner
- ☐ Acrylic paints: off-white and black
- ☐ 15" piece natural jute twine
- ☐ 5" x 6" wood plaque with jute bow
- ☐ Hole punch

Project Note

Refer to photo throughout.

Instructions

1. Cut jute hanger off plaque, cutting close to plaque.

2. Paint back and side edges of plaque with off-white paint.

3. Place paper right side down on flat work surface. Place plaque front side down on top of paper so corner of paper with snowman is even with bottom corner of plaque. Trace around other two sides of plaque.

4. Cut paper along pencil lines. Place paper on top of plaque; mark position of holes on paper and punch with hole punch.

5. Coat front of plaque and wrong side of paper with rubber cement. Let it dry to a dull finish. Carefully position paper on top of plaque, lining up edges precisely.

6. Trim border from remaining paper. Using rubber cement, glue strip of border down left side of plaque and another across top edge.

7. With liner and black paint, write "Let it Snow" on left portion of plaque; add dots to tips of letters.

8. String jute through holes from front to back; knot ends. Tie jute bow to center of hanger. ❧

Craft Stick Snowmen

Posed among your holiday plants, suspended from the trimmed tree or tied with ribbon to holiday gifts ... the uses for these cheerful characters are endless!

Designs by Chris Malone

Let's Begin!

Materials
Set of Three

- ☐ 3 jumbo craft sticks from Forster Inc.
- ☐ Woodsies wooden shapes from Forster Inc.: large (2") oval, 3 small (⅞") teardrops, medium (1") and large (1½") squares, 5 small (⅜") circles, 2 small (⅞") hearts and 2 small (⅞") stars
- ☐ Americana acrylic paints from DecoArt: white wash #DA2, cadmium yellow #DA10, bright green #DA54, lamp black #DA67, true red #DA129 and tangelo orange #DA196
- ☐ Black fine-line permanent marker
- ☐ Matte spray finish
- ☐ 3 (6") pieces (⅜"-wide) multicolored striped grosgrain ribbon
- ☐ 3 (8") pieces white cord or perle cotton
- ☐ Craft drill with small bit
- ☐ Flat paintbrush and small stencil brush
- ☐ Stylus or toothpick
- ☐ Craft cement
- ☐ Craft shears or craft knife

Project Notes
Refer to photo throughout.

Paint all surfaces of wooden pieces.

Let all coats of paint, ink and finish dry between applications.

Instructions
1. Drill hole ½" from one end of each craft stick.

2. Cut large oval in half crosswise to make pieces for two caps; cut a ¼" x 1½" strip from large wooden square for hat brim.

3. Paint wooden pieces as follows: *white wash*—all craft sticks and two small circles; *tangelo orange*—teardrops; *lamp black*—medium square and strip cut in step 2; *true red*—one oval half and both hearts; *cadmium yellow*—both stars; *bright green*—other oval half and three small circles. Add second coats as necessary.

4. *Add face to one end of each jumbo craft stick:* Dip stylus into lamp black and touch to top of craft stick ⅝" below hole for eyes. Mix white wash and true red to make pink for cheeks; dip stencil brush in mixture and remove excess paint on paper towel; tap brush onto face. Using stylus or toothpick dipped in lamp black, add smile of black dots.

5. *Buttonholes:* Using stylus dipped in lamp black, dot two dots in center of each heart, star and bright green circle.

6. Using marker, outline carrot noses, buttons, red and green caps and white circles (pompoms). Draw ribbing along bottom (straight edge) of caps. Spray all pieces with one or two coats of matte finish.

7. Thread each piece of cord through a hole at top of snowman; knot ends.

8. Glue black square to top of one snowman for hat; glue black strip at bottom of hat for brim. Glue red and green caps to remaining snowmen; add white pompom to each.

9. Glue carrot nose to each snowman. Glue heart buttons to snowman with green cap, star buttons to snowman with red cap, and green buttons to snowman with black hat.

10. Wrap ribbon around each snowman's neck and knot off to one side; secure scarves with a dot of glue. ❀

Technique Index

General Instructions

Materials

In addition to the materials listed for each craft, some of the following crafting supplies may be needed to complete your projects. No doubt most of these are already on hand in your "treasure chest" of crafting aids. If not, you may want to gather them before you begin working so that you'll be able to complete each design quickly and without a hitch!

General Crafts

- Scissors
- Pencil
- Ruler
- Tracing paper
- Craft knife
- Heavy-duty craft cutters or wire nippers
- Plenty of newspapers to protect work surface

Painted Items

- Paper towels
- Paper or plastic foam plate or tray to use as a disposable paint palette for holding and mixing paints
- Plastic—a garbage bag, grocery sack, etc.—to protect your work surface
- Container of water or other recommended cleaning fluid for rinsing and cleaning brushes

Fabric Projects

- Iron and ironing board
- Pressing cloth
- Basic sewing notions
- Rotary cutter and self-healing mat
- Air-soluble markers
- Tailor's chalk

Reproducing Patterns & Templates

The patterns provided in this book are shown right side up, as they should look on the finished project; a few oversize patterns that need to be enlarged are clearly marked. Photocopiers with enlarging capabilities are readily available at copy stores and office supply stores. Simply copy the page, setting the photocopier to enlarge the pattern to the percentage indicated.

Patterns that do not need to be enlarged may be reproduced simply by placing a piece of tracing paper or vellum over the pattern in the book, and tracing the outlines carefully with a pencil or other marker.

Once you've copied your pattern pieces, cut them out and use these pieces as templates to trace around. Secure them as needed with pins or pattern weights.

If you plan to reuse the patterns or if the patterns are more intricate, with sharp points, etc., make sturdier templates by gluing the copied page of patterns onto heavy cardboard or template plastic. Let the glue dry, then cut out the pieces with a craft knife.

Depending on the application, it may be preferable to trace the patterns onto the wrong side of the fabric or other material so that no lines will be visible from the front. In this case, make sure you place the right side of the pattern piece against the wrong side of the fabric, paper or other material so that the piece will face the right direction when it is cut out.

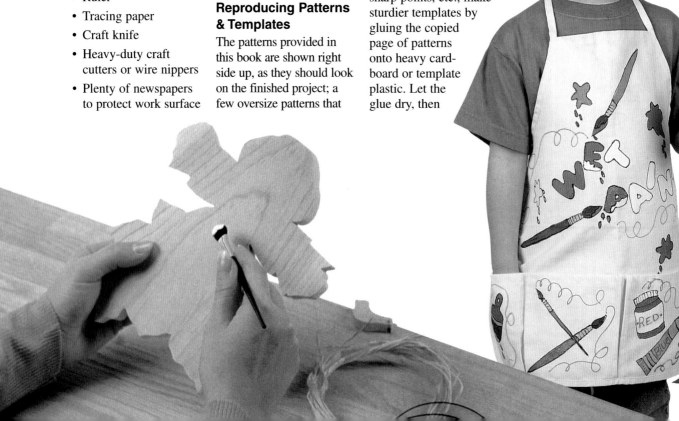

Using Transfer & Graphite Paper

Some projects recommend transferring patterns to wood or another material with transfer or graphite paper. Read the manufacturer's instructions before beginning.

Lay tracing paper over the printed pattern and trace it carefully. Then place transfer paper transfer side down on wood or other material to be marked. Lay traced pattern on top. Secure layers with low-tack masking tape or tacks to keep pattern and transfer paper from shifting while you work.

Using a stylus, pen or other marking implement, retrace the pattern lines using smooth, even pressure to transfer the design onto surface.

Working With Fabrics

Read instructions carefully; take seam allowances into consideration when cutting fabrics.

Pattern markings may be transferred to fabrics with air-soluble markers or tailor's chalk. For permanent markings on fabric, use the specific pens and paints listed with each project. It is always a good idea to test the pen or marker on a scrap of fabric to check for bleeding, etc.

Painted Designs

Disposable paper or plastic foam plates, including supermarket meat trays, make good palettes for pouring and mixing paints. The success of a painted project often depends a great deal on the care taken in the initial preparations, including sanding, applying primer and/or applying a base coat of color. Follow instructions carefully in this regard.

Take special care when painting sections adjacent to each other with different colors; allow the first color to dry so that the second will not run or mix. When adding designs atop a painted base, let the base coat dry thoroughly first.

If you will be mixing media, such as drawing with marking pens on a painted surface, test the process and your materials on scraps to make sure there will be no unsightly running or bleeding.

Keep your work surface and your tools clean. Clean brushes promptly in the manner recommended by the paint manufacturer; many acrylics can be cleaned up with soap and water, while other paints may require a solvent of some kind. Suspend your paintbrushes by their handles to dry to that the fluid drains out completely without bending the bristles.

Work in a well-ventilated area when using paints, solvents or finishes that emit fumes; read product labels thoroughly to be aware of any potential hazards and precautions.

Painting Techniques

Base-coating: Load paintbrush evenly with color by dabbing it on paint can lid, then coat surfaces with one or two smooth, solid coats of paint, letting paint dry between coats.

Comma strokes: Wet #1 script brush; dry on paper towel; dip into paint. Press tip of brush down so that bristles of brush spread out, then slowly pull brush toward you and up onto tip of brush; lift off.

Floating: Dampen brush with water. Touch one side of brush into paint, then sweep brush back and forth on palette to work paint into the brush. Apply the color around the edges of the area you are working on as directed in your painting instructions.

Rouging: Dip dry, round bristle brush in paint and wipe paint off onto paper towel until brush is almost completely dry and leaves no visible brush strokes. Wipe brush across area to be rouged using a circular motion.

Shading: Dip angled shader brush in water and blot lightly once on paper towel, leaving some water in brush. Dip point of brush into paint. Stroke onto palette once or twice to blend paint into water on bristles so that stroke has paint on one side gradually blending to no color on the other side.

Side-loading and high-lighting: Wet flat brush with water; dry on paper towel. Dip corner of brush into paint and brush back and forth on palette until color goes from dark value to light.

Stenciling: Dip dry stencil brush in paint. Wipe brush on paper towel, removing excess paint to prevent seepage under stencil. Brush cutout areas with a circular motion, holding brush perpendicular to surface. When shading, the brush should be almost dry, working only around edges. Use masking tape to hold stencil in place while working.

Wooden Projects

Use extreme caution when using power equipment of any kind, and always wear safety goggles.

Work in a

well-ventilated area when using paints, solvents or finishes that emit fumes; read product labels thoroughly to be aware of any potential hazards and precautions.

Buyer's Guide

Projects in this book were made using products provided by the manufacturers listed below. Look for the suggested products in your local craft- and art-supply stores. If unavailable, contact suppliers below. Some may be able to sell products directly to you; others may be able to refer you to retail sources.

3M
3M Center
Building 304-01-01
St. Paul, MN 55144-1000
(800) 364-3577

Aldastar Pom Beadz
Available through:
Craft Supplies by ArtCove
www.artcove.com/Pompoms/Pombeadz/
pombeadz.shtml

Aleene's
Div. of Duncan Enterprises
5673 E. Shields Ave.
Fresno, CA 93727
(800) 237-2642
www.duncan-enterprises.com

Amaco
American Art Clay Co. Inc.
4717 W. 16th St.
Indianapolis, IN 46222-2598
(317) 244-6871
www.amaco.com

Artistic Wire Ltd.
1210 Harrison Ave.
LaGrange Park, IL 60526
(630) 530-7567
www.artisticwire.com

B&B Products Inc.
19721 N. 98th Ave.
Peoria, AZ 85382
(602) 933-2962

BagWorks Inc.
3301-C S. Cravens Rd.
Fort Worth, TX 76119
(800) 365-7423
www.bagworks.com

Beacon Adhesives/
Signature Marketing
P.O. Box 427
Wyckoff, NJ 07481
(800) 865-7238
www.beacon1.com

Beadalon
www.beadalon.com
(800) 824-9473

The Beadery
P.O. Box 178
Hope Valley, RI 02832
(401) 539-2432

CPE Inc.
541 Buffalo W. Springs Hwy.
Union, SC 29379
(800) 327-0059
www.cpe-felt. com

Crafters Pick by API
520 Cleveland Ave.
Albany, CA 94710
(800) 776-7616
www.crafterspick.com

Crafts Etc!
7717 S.W. 44th St.
Oklahoma City, OK 73179
(800) 888-0321
www.craftsetc.com

Crafty Productions Inc.
2382 Camino Vida Roble, Ste. H
Carlsbad, CA 92009
(760) 929-0052; e-mail: abcrafy@nz.net

C-Thru Ruler Co.
Déjà Views
6 Britton Dr.
Bloomfield, CT 06002-3602
(800) 243-0303
www.cthruruler.com

D&CC
428 S. Zelta
Wichita, KS 67207
(800) 835-3013; e-mail: dcc@feist.com

DMC Corp.
Hackensack Avenue, Bldg. 10A
South Kearny, NJ 07032-4688
(800) 275-4117
www.dmc-usa.com

DMD Industries Inc./
The Paper Reflections Line
1250 ESI Dr.
Springdale, AR 72764
(800) 805-9890
www.dmdind.com

Darice Inc.
Mail-order source: **Bolek's**
330 N. Tuscarawas Ave.
Dover, OH 44622
(330) 364-8878

DecoArt
P.O. Box 386
Stanford, KY 40484
(800) 367-3047
www.decoart.com

Delta Technical Coatings
2550 Pellissier Pl.
Whittier, CA 90601-1505
(800) 423-4135
www.deltacrafts.com

Duncan Enterprises
5673 E. Shields Ave.
Fresno, CA 93727
(800) 237-2642
www.duncan-enterprises.com

Eagle Brush Inc.
(770) 419-4855

EK Success Ltd.
125 Entin Rd.
Clifton, NJ 07014
(800) 524-1349
www.eksuccess.com

EtchAll/
B & B Etching Products Inc.
19721 N. 98th Ave.
Peoria, AZ 85382
(888) 382-4255
www.etchall.com

Fibre-Craft Materials Corp.
Mail-order source: **Kirchen Brothers**
P.O. Box 1016
Skokie, IL 60076
(800)378-5024;
e-mail: kirchenbro@aol.com

Fiskars Inc.
7811 W. Stewart Ave.
Wausau, WI 54401
(800) 950-0203, ext. 1277;
www.fiskars.com

Forster Inc./Diamond Brands
1800 Cloquet
Cloquet, MN 55720
(218) 879-6700;
www.diamondbrands.com/forster.html

Head Starts Enterprises
44-T W. Jefryn Blvd.
Deer Park, NY 11729
(800) 470-6638; www.headstarts.com

Hot Off the Press
1250 N.W. Third
Canby, OR 97013
(503) 266-9102

J & P Coats/
Coats & Clark Inc.
Consumer Service
P.O. Box 12229
Greenville, SC 29612-0229
(800) 648-1479
www.coatsandclark.com

Jones Tones Inc.
33685 United Ave.
Pueblo, CO 81001
(719) 948-0048
www.sales@jonestones.com

Krylon/Sherwin-Williams Co.
Craft Customer Service
101 Prospect Ave. N.W.
Cleveland, OH 44115
(800) 247-3268
www.krylon.com

Kunin Felt Co./Foss Mfg. Co. Inc.
P.O. Box 5000
Hampton, NH 03842-5000
(800) 292-7900
www.kuninfelt.com

Lara's Crafts
590 N. Beach St.
Fort Worth, TX 76111
(800) 232-5272
www.larascrafts.com

Magnetic Specialty Inc.
707 Gilman St.
Marietta, OH 45750
(740) 373-1558
www.magspec.com

Mark Enterprises/
Div. of Stampendous Inc.
(800) 869-0474

Marvy/Uchida of America Corp.
3535 Del Amo Blvd.
Torrance, CA 90503
(800) 541-5877
www.uchida.com

Micron/Sakura of America
30780 San Clemente St.
Hayward, CA 94544
(800) 776-6257
www.gellyroll.com

Nature's Pressed
P.O. Box 212
Orem, UT 84059
(800) 850-2499
www.naturespressed.com

C.M. Offray & Son Inc./
Lion Ribbon Co. Inc.
Route 24, Box 601
Chester, NJ 07930-0601
(800) 555-LION
www.offray.com

One & Only Creations
P.O. Box 2730
Napa, CA 94558
(800) 262-6768
www.oneandonlycreations.com

Paper Reflections/
DMD Industries Inc.
1250 ESI Dr.
Springdale, AR 72764
(800) 805-9890
www.dmdind.com

Pellon Consumer Products
3440 Industrial Dr.
Durham, NC 27704
(919) 620-3916

Plaid Enterprises Inc.
3225 Westech Dr.
Norcross, GA 30092
(800) 842-4197
www.plaidonline.com

Provo Craft
Mail-order source: **Creative Express**
295 W. Center St.
Provo, UT 84601-4436
(800) 563-8679
www.creativeexpress.com

Rubber Stampede Inc.
P.O. Box 246
Berkeley, CA 94701
(800) 632-8386
www.rstampede.com

Sakura Hobby Craft
2444 205th St., A-1
Torrance, CA 90501
(310) 212-7878
e-mail: craftman@earthlink.net

Sculpey III
Polyform Products Co.
1901 Estes Ave.
Elk Grove Village, IL 60007
(847) 427-0020
www.sculpey.com

Scribbles
Div. of Duncan Enterprises
5673 E. Shields Ave.
Fresno, CA 93727
(800) 237-2642
www.duncan-enterprises.com

Seaside Crafter's Edition
Distributed nationwide by
JoAnn's

Speedball Art Products Co.
2226 Speedball Rd.
Statesville, NC 28677
(704) 838-1475

Therm O Web
770 Glenn Ave.
Wheeling, IL 60090
(847) 520-5200
www.thermoweb.com

Tulip
Div. of Duncan Enterprises
5673 E. Shields Ave.,
Fresno, CA 93727
(800) 237-2642
www.duncan-enterprises.com

Uchida of America
3535 Del Amo Blvd.
Torrance, CA 90503
(800) 541-5877
www.uchida.com

V.I.P. Fabrics
1412 Broadway
New York, NY 10018
(800) 847-4064

Walnut Hollow Farms Inc.
1409 St. Rd. 23
Dodgeville, WI 53533-2112
(800) 950-5101
www.walnuthollow.com

The Warm Company
954 E. Union St.
Seattle, WA 98122
(800) 234-WARM
www. warmcompany.com

Wimpole Street Creations
Mail-order source: **Barrett House**
P.O. Box 540585
North Salt Lake, UT 84054-0585
(801) 299-0700
e-mail: wimpole@xmission.com

WoodWorks
4521 Anderson Blvd.
Forth Worth, TX 76117
(817) 582-5230
www.woodworks.com

Wrights
P.O. Box 398
West Warren, MA 01092
(413) 436-7732, ext. 445
www.wrights.com

Yasutomo
490 Eccles Ave.
South San Francisco, CA 94080-1901
(800) 262-6454
www.yasutomo.com